Almshouse Chapels

An Illustrated Gazetteer

Almshouse Chapels

An Illustrated Gazetteer

Canon Dr Raymond Bayley

THE ALMSHOUSE ASSOCIATION

© Canon Dr Raymond Bayley and Third Millennium Publishing Limited

First published in 2013 by Third Millennium Publishing Limited,
a subsidiary of Third Millennium Information Limited.

2–5 Benjamin Street
London
United Kingdom
EC1M 5QL
www.tmiltd.com

ISBN 978 1 908990 09 9

British Library Cataloguing in Publication Data
A CIP catalogue record for this book is available from the British Library.

Design: www.carrdesignstudio.com
Production: Bonnie Murray
Repro: Studio Fasoli, Verona, Italy
Printed by Printer Trento, Italy

III

THIRD MILLENNIUM
PUBLISHING, LONDON

Contents

Preface

ALMSHOUSE CHAPELS come in many shapes and sizes. They date from different periods and serve various functions. Some are ancient, such as the ruined Hospital of St Leonard in York which traces its foundation to the tenth century; others very new, as is the Chapel of St Bruno recently dedicated in the nursing wing of the Charterhouse in London. In many chapels, such as that of St John's Hospital without the Barrs in Lichfield, worship is offered daily; others are no longer used for their primary purpose and have been converted into community rooms, or additional almshouses. Some, like the magnificent medieval church of St Cross at Winchester are large, others, like the chapel of William Penny's Hospital at Lancaster, are very small. Most chapels are situated centrally within the complex of almshouse buildings, although the chapel of the House of God at Ewelme is situated within the adjacent church of St Mary. Nearly all almshouse chapels are of Anglican foundation, although the Quaker meeting house at Michael Holgate's Hospital, Margate and the Congregational chapel at Joseph Crossley's Homes in Halifax are exceptions. In many cases, almshouse chapels now welcome ecumenical worship alongside the tradition of their original foundation.

Since I began my study of almshouse chapels in 2005 I have traced more than two hundred, and have enjoyed the pleasure of visiting more than a half of these. I am extremely grateful to all those trustees and clerks who have sent information, and where possible have spared the time to show me around their chapels. In the process I have met some very interesting and well-informed people as well as admiring a great number of outstanding buildings.

I particularly wish to thank Major General Anthony Leask, formerly Director of the Almshouse Association, who encouraged me to embark upon this project, and his successor Lieutenant Colonel Anthony De Ritter and his staff, who have been extremely supportive and helpful at every stage of the work.

It would be premature to imagine that this book presents a final or definitive account of all almshouse chapels. Doubtless there are some which have escaped my notice, or of which more deserves to be said than is given here. But I hope at least to have given a broad picture which future authors may correct and enlarge upon.

RB July 2013

ABERFORD, West Yorkshire

The Gascoigne Almshouses.

These almshouses, built of white limestone in a Victorian High Gothic style, were founded by the Gascoigne sisters in 1844 and are now used as a private residence. The stone chapel of 1844 has a high central tower and many gables and pinnacles and is situated in the central block opposite the dining room.

Howson* 67, 149. Pl.21. Pevsner/Ratcliffe 1967: 69.

ACTON, London

Goldsmiths' Almshouses.

The famous goldsmith John Perryn, who lived for a time in East Acton Lane, left his estate to the Goldsmiths' Company. On the land bequeathed to the Goldsmiths, the original almshouses were built in 1811, with others added in 1838. One of the main rooms, furnished with a stucco pediment and centrally situated, was converted into a chapel.

Howson* 129.

Left: Interior of Royal Hospital chapel, Chelsea, by Wren, 1681. See page 15.

Below: Chapel interior at Lady Anne Clifford's Hospital , Appleby

AMPTHILL, Bedfordshire

Dr Crosse Hospital of the University of Oxford.

The almshouses were founded by Dr John Crosse in 1690. The building, in Wren style, including a chapel, was built between 1705 and 1712. It has chequered brickwork, original windows and a cupola. The chapel contains a two-decker reading desk and the original stalls and panelling, A set of leather fire buckets is marked with the date 1719. Daily services ceased in the 1930s. The hospital was conveyed to the Church Army in the 1950s and has recently been sold.

Howson* 110.

APPLEBY, Cumbria

Lady Anne Clifford's Hospital.

The hospital was founded by Lady Anne Clifford in 1651. The chapel is contained within the main structure. It has an East window of two round arched lights, a pulpit with 17th-century panelling and benches with simply-shaped ends.

Corry. Howson* 113. Pevsner 1967: 221.

ASHBOURNE, Derbyshire

Cooper's Almshouses.

These almshouses of 1800 are now in private ownership. They are associated with an adjoining United Reformed Chapel.

Pevsner/Williamson 2002: 65. Hallett 50. Howson* 115.

AUDLEY END, Essex

The College of St Mark.

In 1258 Bishop Hugh de Balsham dedicated a hospital attached to Walden Abbey, a Benedictine foundation. When the Abbey was dissolved at the Reformation, the

A

hospital became derelict. Early in the 17th century, when the Earl of Suffolk was building the great mansion of Audley End, he converted the old hospital into almshouses and included a chapel in the central block between the two courtyards. By 1836 the old chapel had been converted into a barn, and part of it was demolished. In 1950 Lord Braybrooke gave the buildings to the Diocese of Chelmsford to accommodate retired clergy. The demolished part of the chapel was rebuilt and rededicated by the Bishop of Chelmsford in 1951. At this time the building was named 'St Mark's College'. By 1990 the college was considered no longer suitable for retired clergy owing to its isolated location. The Diocese converted it into a residential centre for youth work. It was dedicated for this purpose in 1994.

Howson* 120.

BARNET, Hertfordshire

The Leathersellers' Barnet Charities.

Although the almshouses were built in 1837, the present chapel was not built until 1926. A small earlier chapel had ceased to be used by 1899 and become a meeting room. The chapel was the gift of the Master at the time, Frederick Lionel Dove, in memory of his uncle, Lionel John Prime, a Leatherseller, and his mother, Marian Ann Dove. The chapel is built in the Gothic style, in harmony with the rest of the almshouse complex, and was officially opened by the Bishop of London on 9 June 1926. The chapel interior is relatively plain with oak fittings. There is a carved reredos which contains a painting by the Scottish artist Peter Alexander Hay (1866–1952) showing

Christ in the Garden after the Resurrection with Mary Magdalen and Salome. The chapel is still used for monthly services, as well as other services on special occasions. Weddings and funerals have occasionally taken place there in recent years. There is an annual Christmas Carol service in the chapel which is attended by the Master of the Company and many senior Leathersellers and staff, as well as by most of the almshouse residents.

Pevsner/Cherry 1977 31. Farrell.

BATH, Somerset

Partis College.

The almshouses were built in 1820 in the style of Downing College in Cambridge. They include a college chapel whose entrance is classical in design while the sanctuary is decorated in a richly ornate style. The coat of arms of Lady Partis is to be seen in one of the windows. Services are regularly held, and all the residents are expected to attend.

Brochure.

Left: Partis College chapel, Bath.

Left: St John's Hospital, Bath.

Below: The Duchess of Cornwall at St John's Hospital.

B

St John's Hospital.

The earliest charter of the Hospital of St John Baptist is dated *c.*1180. Its chapel, Romanesque in style, also served as a chantry. In 1572 the nearby church of St Michael by the Baths was annexed to the hospital, but this church had become ruinous by 1600. St John's chapel was restored and given a wooden bell tower in 1580, but was described as being 'very ruinous' by 1717 when it was rebuilt in a restrained baroque style. A further restoration on the same site commenced in 1880. New windows by Ward and Hughes were installed, a new floor and apse added, new pine benches fitted, the pulpit replaced by a reading desk and a new entrance made to the vestry. At this time the chapel was re-dedicated to St Michael.

The chapel of St Mary Magdalen was given by Walter Hussey to the Bishop of Bath *c.*1100, and was used for some time as a leper hospital. Between 1483 and 1499 John Cantlow, Prior of Bath, rebuilt this chapel. It was refitted as a chapel of ease by the Revd Duel Taylor in 1760. A tower and battlemented east end were added in the early 19th century. The chapel had its stained glass shattered and its roof burned as a result of bombing in 1942. It was re-roofed in 1947, and a new east window designed by Michael Farrer Bell depicting the three medieval foundations (St Catherine, St John Baptist and St Mary Magdalene) was installed some time later. *Manco. Hallett 43.*

BAWTRY, South Yorkshire

The Hospital of St Mary Magdalene.

This hospital was founded in 1280 for the benefit of the sick and poor. It was extended in 1390 by Robert Morton, who endowed Nostell Priory to provide a chaplain in perpetuity to say prayers for himself and his wife. The hospital chapel continued to serve as a chantry throughout the 15th century. It survived the Reformation, but by 1580 it had fallen into a ruinous state and services were no longer being conducted regularly. The chapel was repaired in the early 17th century, but again fell into a poor state and by 1834 was being used as a carpenter's shop. It was restored in 1839, and in the mid 20th century it was acquired by the Bawtry Freemasons' Lodge.

Howson* 148.

BEAMSLEY, Yorkshire
Beamsley Hospital.

Beamsley Hospital was founded as almshouses for local women in 1593 by Lady Margaret Clifford. It was completed around 1650–60 by her daughter Lady Anne Clifford. It has a circular chapel lit by clerestory windows. Seven rooms radiate out from the chapel. The building was restored and altered in 1961 and is now owned by the Landmark Trust.

Corry. Hallett 34, 35, 53. Howson 29, 35. Howson* 107, 146. Pl.13.

Below: Beamsley Hospital.

B

BERWICK, Shropshire

Berwick Almshouses.

The almshouses were founded in 1672 by the will of Sir Samuel Jones. They were situated in the grounds of Berwick House together with the chapel. Sir Samuel bequeathed £300 for the repair of the chapel and £80 a year to maintain a minister. The almshouses were sold in 1699 to Richard Hosier, who was the subject of a court order in 1720 ordering him to repair the chapel. This was done in 1723 by Thomas Powis, to whom Hosier had, in the meantime, sold the almshouses. A west tower was added in 1731. The chapel has an arched west doorway and a south porch with arched entry. The east end with its transepts with an eastern gable and fanciful windows dates from 1892–94. There are box pews and a west gallery. The pulpit dates from *c.*1675.

Pevsner 2002: 73, 74. Watts 32, 35.

BEVERLEY, North Yorkshire

The Hospital of St Mary the Blessed Virgin.

In 1400 the King licensed a Guild belonging to St Mary's Church to acquire land to build a hospital. The hospital was built in 1433–34 on the east side of the North Bar and by 1463 it had its own chapel. In 1557–58 it was acquired by the Town Council who maintained a Maison Dieu there. The building was demolished in 1772.

Howson 34. Hopkins 113, 141.

The Hospital of St Giles.

This house existed by the late 12th century. It was annexed to Warter Priory in 1277. The hospital, together with its church and churchyard, was dissolved in 1536. It was sold in 1753 and Lairgate Hall was built on its site.

Hopkins 56, 141, 155, 217.

The Hospital of St Nicholas.

The house was in existence by 1287 and was sometimes known as the friary. A chantry in the hospital chapel was mentioned from 1311 and endowed in 1378. The hospital was suppressed at the Dissolution. Remnants of the building were still evident in the moat around the Minster close in the 19th century.

Hopkins 114, 141.

The Hospital of The Holy Trinity.

The hospital and its chantry chapel were founded by John of Aike before 1397. After dissolution the building was a maison dieu and eventually a prison. It was demolished in 1810.

Hopkins 141, 165.

The Hospital of St John the Baptist.

This hospital was first mentioned in 1440. It had a chapel and a chantry. After dissolution a maison dieu was maintained on the site.

Hopkins 141, 165.

The Hospital of St John the Evangelist.

This hospital was mentioned in 1444. It was granted by the Crown to the Corporation in 1585 for maintenance as a maison dieu.

Hopkins 114.

B

BLACKHEATH, London

Morden College.

The chapel was built as an integral part of the main college building in 1695 and consecrated on 29 September 1701. The royal arms of William III can be seen above the reredos. This reredos is carved with cherubs and festoons. The building contains the original oak furnishings, high pews fitted with doors, and an elegant six-sided 'tulip' pulpit reached by an ornamental staircase, the whole surmounted by a heavy inlaid canopy with a cornice carved with leaves. The east window contains 16th- and 17th-century glass made in England, Holland and Germany and presented by a Trustee, Lord Melville, in 1850. During the 20th century the plain glass of the side windows was replaced by commemorative stained glass including windows honouring Sir John and

Lady Morden. The woodwork in the porch is contemporary and includes some fine carving in the manner of Grinling Gibbons.

Guide book. Howson 111–112. Howson* 51.

BRADFORD, West Yorkshire

The Bradford Tradesmen's Homes.

The chapel is situated in the centre of the northern block (1870). It has a projected canted front and a crowning clock turret; a shafted doorway with lunette and wing from arch; a 2-light colonetted window in the gable. The two stone alpacas flanking the entrance come from Sir Titus Salt's home. Stained glass windows were donated in memory of Sir Titus Salt, Henry Harris, Benjamin Briggs Popplewell, James Rhodes, Thomas Buck, Isaac Wright and Henry Brown. A clock was donated in 1897 in memory of Mr James Drummond. The

Below: The chapel, Morden College, Blackheath.

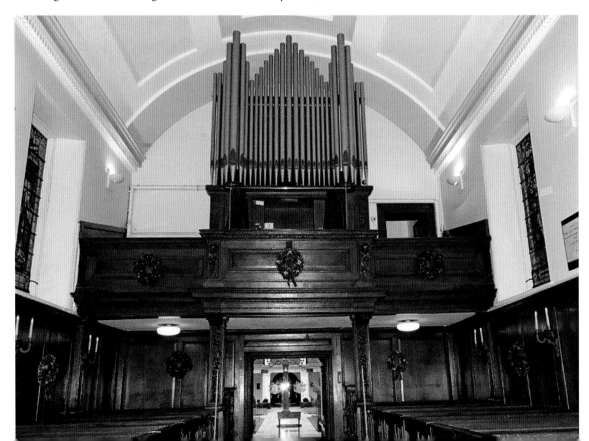

Above and right:
Chapel exterior and interior, the Bradford Tradesmen's Homes.

chapel is given over to the use of the community of residents who hold various functions on a regular basis and services at Christmas, Easter and Harvest Festival.
Annual Report. Corry. Hallett 23. Howson 146, 152. Howson* 67. Askew.

BRADFORD ON AVON, Wiltshire

St Catherine's Almshouses.
At their original foundation these almshouses were supplied with a chapel on the town bridge. Its existence is confirmed on a map of 1770 and there is reference to it in a Charity Commission report of 1824 which states that by this date the bell had been removed to Winsley church. Only slight remnants of this chapel now remain.
Website.

BRAY, Berkshire

Jesus Hospital.
William Goddard in his will of 1609 left land upon which almshouses were to be erected. This Trust was administered by the Worshipful Company of Fishmongers, and the almshouses were built between 1623 and 1628, the chapel being consecrated in 1626. The windows in the sanctuary contain several coats of arms, including most prominently those of the Fishmongers. The chapel contains a picture by Frederick Walker, 'The Harbour of Refuge', depicting Jesus Hospital in the early 20th century, as well as a memorial window to Walker erected by the Fishmongers' Company in 1908. A list of chaplains up to recent times is displayed. The screen was presented in 1907 but appears to be much older; possibly it was brought from elsewhere. A tapestry featuring the arms of the Worshipful Company of Fishmongers is thought to date from the 1970s, as do the hassocks. When the almshouses were modernised in 1986 a vestry was provided alongside the chapel. A fortnightly service is held in the chapel by the Vicar of Bray.
Website.

B

BRISTOL

John Barstaple's Almshouse.
These almshouses were founded in the early 19th century. The chapel was originally large, but much of it has been converted into a common room. A small worship area is regularly used, containing large floor brasses of the Barstaple family.

John Foster's Almshouses.
The chapel was built 'in honour of God and the three Kings of Cologne' in 1484. The purported remains of the Three Kings had been held in Milan since the 4th century but had been removed to Cologne Cathedral in 1164. The chapel contains a brass chandelier dated 1696, made by John Spooner. It is thought to be the earliest example of a Bristol-made brass chandelier. The chapel underwent renovation in 1883 and again in 1962 when the Bristol sculptor Ernest Pascoe carved the statues of the Three Kings situated in the niches on the front elevation. At the same time, Patrick Pollen of Dublin designed a new East Window depicting the Three Kings making their offerings to Christ. The baby Jesus is represented as symbolically crucified on Mary's lap. A candlelit Communion service was held annually on the Feast of Epiphany, 6 January. Foster's Almshouse has recently been sold, and the chapel awaits disposal. The ancient coat of arms and other fittings have been removed, and are to be installed in a Foster's Memorial Area at the new almshouses which have replaced the city site.

D. Jones. Hallett 36, 54. Howson* 109.

Above: Chapel façade, John Foster's Almshouses, Bristol.

Colston's Almshouses.
Founded in 1691, these almshouses have a three-bay chapel. A short weekly service is conducted by the Almshouse Chaplain each Wednesday.

Howson* 109. Collins.

BROMLEY, Kent

Bromley and Sheppard's Colleges.
Bromley College was founded by John Warner, Bishop of Rochester, in 1666 as almshouses for clergy widows. It was built in 1670–72 to a design by Thomas Hardwick. Nothing remains of the first chapel, nor of the second chapel which replaced it in 1701. This chapel, like its predecessor, was found to be too small, and so it was rebuilt in 1863 in an Early Decorated style. This new chapel was consecrated by Archbishop Longley in 1864. The eight stained glass windows depict biblical incidents involving women. At the west end of the chapel are four window spaces in which have been painted the coats of arms of some of the college benefactors. The chapel contains two portraits, one of John Warner and the other of Bishop Zachary Pearce. The Compton organ was added in 1934, and at the same time a vestry was created in the crypt. On the chapel wall is an embroidered sampler commemorating Mrs Sophia Sheppard, who founded Sheppard's College in 1840, and inscribed 'From her Five adopted daughters'. The pews are arranged in collegiate style. The chaplain's and treasurer's stalls have double-pitched canopies above.

Gough.

B

BROMLEY-BY-BOW, London

Drapers' Almshouses.

The chapel and four of the almshouses date from 1706. The arms of the Drapers' Company adorn the front of the central chapel.

Website.

BRUTON, Somerset

Hugh Sexey's Hospital.

The Hospital was founded under the will of Hugh Sexey, Auditor of the Exchequer to Elizabeth I and James I. Hugh Sexey may have been born in Bruton, but an alternative account places his origins in Bristol. He died in 1619. In 1638 his Trustees erected a hospital on part of the estates at Bruton. The Jacobean chapel in the courtyard contains pews, a pulpit and a reading desk, all of carved oak. Services are held there on five days of the week, the order of service being based on the 1662 Book of Common Prayer. The chapel has its own choir. The roof of the chapel was repaired with financial assistance from English Heritage between 1995 and 2005.

Howson* 138. Parfitt.

Below: The Sandham Memorial Chapel.

BURGHCLERE, Berkshire

The Sandham Memorial Chapel.

The chapel is situated next to the almshouses. It is now in the care of the National Trust. The artist Stanley Spencer spent six years painting the murals in the chapel. The paintings reflect Spencer's experiences at the Beaufort Hospital in Bristol and then in Salonika and Macedonia during the First World War. The almshouses and chapel were given to the National Trust in 1947. The residents remained until the 1980s, when they were moved to alternative accommodation so that the almshouses might be used as offices and staff accommodation.

Website. Paton.

CALVERHALL, Shropshire

Calverhall Almshouses.

The almshouses were founded in 1738 by the Honourable Katherine Kerr. A chapel was originally provided, and can be seen in

C

a picture painted in 1791. This ceased to be used when Calverhall Church was built onto the north end of the almshouses in 1872–78.

Watts 46–47. Pevsner 2002: 93.

CANTERBURY, Kent

The Hospital of St Thomas the Martyr, Eastbridge.

The Chantry Chapel of Our Lady was built *c.*1180. The arch separating the main part of the chapel from the sanctuary dates from the 14th century. The chapel was closed in 1547 and restored in 1969, when an icon of Our Lady was placed over the altar. The beam on the altar side of the arch comes from an old inn, The Saracen's Head in Burgate, and was placed there during the 1969 restoration.

The Pilgrims' Chapel was built in 1190. The fine woodwork of the roof dates from *c.*1285. The chapel assumed its present form in the 14th century. The sanctus bell within an oak bell-cage in the ceiling was cast in 1727. The altar stands against a wall decorated with a reconstruction of the 13th century mural in the Refectory. This was painted by Professor Tristram, as was the portrait of Eadwine which is situated on the west wall. The chapel also contains some old pews, carved chairs for the Archbishop and the Master, and a set of ancient stalls with misericords dating from the early 15th century. This chapel was used as a schoolroom from 1569 to 1880 and was restored to its original use in 1927.

Hayes/Pinnock/White. Ingram Hill/Lyle 23–32.

The Hospital of St John Baptist, Northgate.

The hospital was founded *c.*1085. The shape of the buildings seems to have been a Tau cross of which the original chapel formed the lower part looking east with two naves and probably two apses. The ruins of this building can be seen to the west of the present chapel.

The present chapel appears to have been built in the later Middle Ages. It has a handsome perpendicular east window. The font, with a curious Jacobean cover like a table leg, is of early medieval date. The Royal Arms hangs on the wall just above it, with the date 1607 above the arms of George II, suggesting that it was repainted a century or more after its erection. There is a 17th-century silver chalice. The patronal festival of the hospital is kept on 24 June, the Nativity of St John Baptist.

Ingram Hill/Lyle1–11. Ingram Hill. Howson 39. Howson 84, 124.*

The Hospital of St Nicolas, Harbledown.

The Church of St Nicolas ceased to be a parish church and was designated as an almshouse church in 1934. The west door, tower and much of the nave are Norman. The north aisle was added in the 12th century. The windows in the chancel are 14th century and contain glass of that period. There are some 13th-century stalls. A south chapel dedicated to St Thomas of Canterbury was added in the 14th century. The roof is also of the 14th century. The tower has four bells. The font is medieval.

Ingram Hill/Lyle 11–22. Ingram Hill. Howson 20, 39. Howson 22, 144. Pl.1.*

Maynard and Cotton's Spital.

This hospital, possibly founded in the reign of Henry II, was dedicated to Our Lady and had a chapel in the middle. It has one large window at the south end. The arms of Queen Anne are inside the chapel over the door. There is a small wooden candelabra, and a bell in a turret outside. An inscription over the exterior door records the rebuilding of the chapel in 1708. Another inscription mentions repairs in 1617.

Ingram Hill/Lyle 32–35.

Right: Queen Anne's coat of arms, Maynard and Cotton's Spital, Canterbury.

Below: The chapel, Maynard and Cotton's Spital.

C

Sir John Boys' Hospital of Jesus in Northgate.
A Warden was commissioned in 1599
to 'say publicly prayers Morning and
Evening in the chapel of the Hospital'.
The chapel was splendidly restored and
furnished with a new east window and
furniture in 1964.
Ingram Hill/Lyle 41, 42.

The Poor Priests' Hospital.
The hospital is thought to have been
founded in 1218. The building presently
serves as the Museum of Canterbury.
A surviving building which runs to
the east in Stour Street appears to have
been the chapel.
Ingram Hill/Lyle 52. Howson* 124.

Opposite: Greyfriars' Chapel, Canterbury.

Greyfriars' Chapel.
This was the first Franciscan house in
England, established in 1224. It both served
the neighbourhood and provided lodgings
for those passing to and from London and
the continent. The house was rebuilt in stone
from 1267. The great church has by now
disappeared, and the building which serves
as the chapel was probably the guesthouse.
The friary was suppressed in 1538. It then
became a private house. The main restoration
of the Greyfriars Chapel was undertaken in
the early 1920s, under the auspices of the
then owner, Major James, and his architect
Mr R.H. Goodsell of Whitstable. The upper
rooms were furnished as a chapel, and the
Dean and Chapter of Canterbury Cathedral
became the owners in 1958. In 2000 the
chapel was sold to Eastbridge Hospital.
Taylor, Carey.

CARLETON-IN-CRAVEN, North Yorkshire

Spence's Hospital.

The hospital was founded by Ferrand Spence in 1698. It has a chapel at the far end of its courtyard.

Howson 98–99.*

CASTLE RISING, Norfolk

The Hospital of the Holy and Undivided Trinity.

The almshouses were endowed by Henry Howard, Earl of Northampton, in his will in 1614 and were constructed during the period 1614–23. The Chapel is contemporary with the buildings, although with a later upgrade in the early 20th century. The Sisters, as the residents

Above: The Hospital of the Holy and Undivided Trinity, Castle Rising.

Below: Harvey's and Jubilee Homes, Chard.

of the almshouses, were required to worship in the chapel twice a day. Around the perimeter at roof level are shields and symbols of the Howards and local history. The chapel houses a wooden altar set of cross and candelabra by Voysey.

Howson 102, Hallett 54. Howson⁴ 132. Waite

CHARD, Somerset

Harvey's and Jubilee Homes.

These homes have as origin the will of Richard Harvey dated 1663, but they became dilapidated and were rebuilt in 1841. A Common Room was built sometime later, in 1903. The building is now used as a studio for the talking newspaper for the blind.

Prior.

CHARNOCK RICHARD, Lancashire

The Frances Darlington Almshouses.

The almshouses with their chapel were founded by James Darlington in 1898 in memory of his wife Frances Darlington. Services in the chapel were discontinued in the 1980s but in 1996 were restored with weekly services of Holy Communion. The chapel contains a memorial to Frances Darlington, a window by Kempe in memory of Frances Darlington's governess, Mary Anna Lord, a marble fireplace and an oak library chest. The altar is an original almshouse chest of drawers. The wall tiling, the roof timbers and the parquet floor are all original. The original mosaic tiles in the porch had suffered damage, but were salvaged by the Day School. A framed mosaic was constructed and can be seen hanging on a wall in the school. The original bell, which used to be tolled every evening at 9pm, was electrified in the late 1990s.

Stewart.

CHATHAM, Kent

St Bartholomew's Hospital.

This hospital, situated on the boundary between Chatham and Rochester, was founded in 1078 by Gundulph, Bishop of Rochester, for the 'poor and leperous'. The stone nave and chancel of the chapel, built in 1124, are the only surviving remnants of the original buildings. The chapel was restored by Sir George Gilbert Scott in 1896, with the addition of a north aisle and vestry. The remaining buildings of the hospital were replaced in the 19th century. The chapel is presently out of use and awaiting sale.

Howson 124.*

CHELSEA, London

The Royal Hospital.

The hospital and chapel, designed by Sir Christopher Wren, were founded in 1681.

The chapel stands in Figure Court, the principal court. It was designed to accommodate about 500 people, all the staff and pensioners, and rises 42' high. The wainscotting and pews are by Sir Charles Hopson, the leading joiner of his day and deputy Clerk of Works at the Royal Hospital from 1691–98. The choir stalls are modern additions. Backs have been fitted to the benches, and the three-decker pulpit has been dismantled to make the existing pulpit and reading desk. Apart from these alterations the original plan has been maintained. The plaster work was carried out by Henry Margetts. The carving is by

C

William Emmett, Master Carver before Grinling Gibbons and William Morgan. The organ case is the work of Renatus Harris, but his organ has been replaced by a modern instrument. The painting of the Resurrection in the half-dome of the apse is by Sebastiano Ricci, assisted by his nephew Marco, and dates from 1714. The work was probably paid for, as a donation to the Royal Hospital, by Queen Anne. The Hospital's magnificent silver gilt altar plate was made by Ralph Leete and is hallmarked 1667–68. It comprises a large alms dish, a pair of candlesticks with baluster stems, a salver, three flagons, four chalices and patens, and a straining spoon. The altar cross, the font, and the coat of arms on the front of the organ loft date from 1955–56. One of the original service books has been preserved. The chapel was consecrated in 1691, and compulsory services were held twice daily. Today they are normally confined to Sunday morning services before which the In-Pensioners parade in Figure Court.

Hallett 54. Howson* 48. Website.

CHESTER, Cheshire

The Hospital of St John.

This was founded around 1190. In about 1240 the brethren were given permission to build a chapel known as St John-without-the-Northgate or Little St John. In 1316 the responsibility for maintaining the services and almsgiving of the hospital passed to Birkenhead Priory. This arrangement was unsuccessful, and an inquiry of 1341 found that the chapel and hospital buildings were not adequately roofed. The commissioners who visited Chester in 1553 to list Church

goods found 'nothing worth selling' here. In February 1644 all stone buildings of the hospital and chapel were demolished during the Civil War. At the Restoration the Wardenship was granted to Colonel Roger Whitley, who is said to have rebuilt the hospital. New buildings were erected on the site in 1717, including the Bluecoat Charity School. A new chapel was built in the southern wing. The school and almshouses were rebuilt in 1854. The Bluecoat School finally closed in 1949. Its buildings are presently occupied by the history department of the University of Chester, the former chapel serving as the reception area. A small cross and bell can still be seen on its roof. It has a chalice of 1641, a paten by Richard Richardson I (1716), a paten of *c.*1730, and a chalice by John Robins (1781).

Pevsner/Hubbard 2003: 161, 162. Website.

CHICHESTER, Sussex

St Mary's Hospital.

The hospital is thought to have been founded in the second half of the 12th century, the almshouses being incorporated into the chapel building. It was refounded on its present site after 1290. The chapel has survived with very little alteration to its original state. A large stone arch marks the entrance, beneath which is the 13th-century screen. The east window, depicting the Blessed Virgin Mary, was unblocked and restored in 1880 and again in 1943 after bomb damage. The other windows are fine examples of Decorated tracery. On the south side are the original stone piscina and sedilia, both finely carved and partly restored. The rood beam has some

Above left and below: St Mary's Hospital, Chichester, Sussex.

Above right: St Mary's Church, Cleeton St Mary, Shropshire.

17th-century decoration added beneath it. Below the screen and round the side walls are 24 stalls with misericords. These are by different carvers and are in varying styles, one carving representing the Green Man. In 1728 it was recorded that the poor were diligently to attend Morning Prayer.

Munby. Howson 40. Howson* 78–79. Macdougall 98.

Above: Misericords at St Mary's Hospital, Chichester, Sussex.

The Cawley Almshouses.

Originally named St Bartholomew's Hospital, these almshouses were founded by William Cawley, a staunch Parliamentarian, Governor of Chichester, who was among the signatories to the death warrant of King Charles I. In consequence of this, his almshouses were occupied by the

Above: The Hospital of the Holy and Undivided Trinity, Clun, Shropshire.

St Mary in 1883. The almshouse residents were expected to attend the church daily unless prevented by illness.

Watts 50. Pevsner 2002: 105.

CLUN, Shropshire

The Hospital of the Holy and Undivided Trinity.

The hospital and chapel were founded in 1607 by Henry Howard, Earl of Northampton. The residents were required to attend the chapel at 9am and 3pm each day. Archdeacon Plymley's Visitation of 1793 confirmed that this was still the case. The chapel is gable ended with lancet windows. It was rebuilt in the mid-19th century but retains its original furnishings.

Hallett 54. Pevsner 2002: 225–226. Watts 53–57.

COBHAM, Kent

New College.

This was originally a chantry college for priests, but is now a foundation for retired people.

Hallett 54.

COLCHESTER, Essex

The Chapel of St Helen.

The chapel was first built by King Offa in the 8th century within the ruined walls of the Roman theatre. It was restored by the Normans at the building of Colchester Castle in 1076. Early in the 14th century it became an almshouse chapel when John of Colchester founded a chantry with attached almshouse. This continued until King Henry VIII closed the chantry, almshouse and chapel in 1539. The chapel was used for secular purposes until 1880 when the Round family purchased it and employed

Royalist army under William Walker in 1642. Cawley fled to Switzerland at the Restoration and died there. His son brought the body back to Chichester where it was laid to rest under the almshouse chapel. The hospital had no connection to the established Church, being vested instead with the city corporation. From 1753 it was used as a workhouse. Today the white brick chapel, easily recognised by its original door and window, bellcote and bell, has been incorporated into a modern housing development, Cawley Towers.

Macdougall 63–68, 75, 99.

CLEETON ST MARY, Shropshire

The Pardoe Almshouses.

George Pardoe founded a church, school and almshouses close together in Cleeton

Above: The Chapel of St Helen, Colchester.

Below: Winsley's Charity, Colchester.

William Butterfield to restore it. Since 2000 St Helen's Chapel has been an Orthodox Parish Church.
Website.

Winsley's Charity.

The original almshouses and chapel were erected in accordance with Arthur Winsley's will of 1726. The work of converting the original farmhouse into the first twelve dwellings and chapel was commenced in 1734. Arthur Winsley stipulated that a 'Good Preacher' should be paid to preach a sermon every New Year, and the tradition continues to this day. The chapel is also used for social gatherings and activities and for residents' meetings.
Website. Dale.

CORSHAM, Wiltshire

Corsham Almshouses.

The almshouses were completed in 1668. Among the orders made by Lady Margaret Hungerford at this time were, that in addition to regular attendance at Corsham Church, 'I do likewise appoint that everyone of these poor people shall constantly be present every Week Day at the prayers twice in a day at the School House and likewise at the Repetition of the Sermon every Sunday in the Evening either at the School House or at the Great Mansion House in Corsham aforesaid upon pain to Forfeit for every default therein twelve pence.' The schoolroom is furnished as a chapel with a pulpit, box pews, and a gallery. A visitor of *c.*1925 described the chapel as she found it at that time: 'She admired the old two-decker pulpit, the oak pews and desks ranged along the wall, the richly carved gallery in which the oak had been harmoniously mellowed by that supreme artist, Time, and the sense of light and space afforded by the windows.' The room has retained almost all of its original features. It is

Above: Chapel interior, Corsham Almshouses.

C

divided from the entrance by a timber-framed screen with two oak-framed square-headed doorways. The front of the gallery is Jacobean and features six balusters with Ionic capitals. In the centre are two tablets with curled decoration depicting the Hungerford and Halliday arms. On the east wall is a large stone fireplace. The floor, now raised and with narrow floorboards, was probably originally stone-flagged. On either side of the pulpit are life-sized carved wooden hands, the clasped fingers of which form sockets for holding candles. A chair with curved armrests and turned front legs with a footrest is set into the front of the pulpit. The box pews would have been occupied by the almshouse residents, and the benches by the scholars during times of worship. However, the chapel has not been used as a place of prayer for well over a hundred years. There is a bell tower above the main entrance.

Leaflet. Hird 103, 186–191, 199, 206, 209.

COVENTRY, West Midlands

The Bablake Hospital.

The hospital was originally founded by the Holy Trinity Fraternity in the 12th century, along with a fine church. It was re-founded by Thomas Bond in 1507. Only the Guild Church, situated to the south of the almshouses, now survives as the Parish Church of St John. It is of red sandstone with a tower nave of two bays, all under a tunnel vault. The windows are long and thin, of two lights and straight headed. The church is Perpendicular in style, restored in 1877 by Sir Giles Gilbert Scott. The screen of 1886 is by John Oldryd Scott. The stained glass in the south aisle is by Kempe (1896). Among the plate are a paten of 1650, a chalice and paten of 1739–40, and a chalice of 1845.

Howson* 28. Pevsner/Wedgwood 1966: 261–62.

COWLEY, Oxford

St Bartholomew's Hospital.

This was a leper hospital founded and endowed by Henry I in 1126. It was set in a grove near Cowley Marsh with its own well a mile outside the walls of the City of Oxford. Indigent sick were also cared for in the hospital, so that it became part almshouse. In 1329 Edward III transferred the hospital to Oriel College who not only administered it as an almshouse but also offered it to their scholars so that they could enjoy 'the use of wholesome air in times of pestilential sickness'. The chapel was rebuilt at this time. By the 16th century the hospital was also being used as a refuge from the plague. The buildings suffered badly in the Civil War and were rebuilt by Oriel College in 1649. The chapel, which had been used as a stable by Cromwell's soldiers, was re-roofed. Over the next 200 years the hospital was not well maintained, but during the cholera epidemic in 1832 the Board of Health turned the hospital into a convalescent home. The chapel fell into disuse, but the second Vicar of Cowley St John, Fr William Scott, instigated action to restore the chapel as a place of worship. St Bartholomew's Chapel was gifted to the parish in 1913 by Oriel College and has been in regular use since. Amongst those using the chapel have been Archimandrite Nicholas and the Russian Orthodox congregation, from 1941 until 1949. There are now regular parish services in the chapel, commonly known as Bartlemas, and it is also used for concerts and occasional exhibitions.

Website.

CROYDON, Surrey

The Hospital of the Holy Trinity.

These almshouses were founded in 1596 by Archbishop John Whitgift. A chapel is situated in the north-east corner. Every Friday morning the resident who has lived longest in the almshouses rings the chapel bell for the stipend ceremony. On the north wall of the small chapel is a tablet containing quotations from the Church Fathers. The south wall shows the Ten Commandments flanked by splendidly decorated figures of Moses and Aaron. On the west wall is a portrait of Archbishop Whitgift.

Hallett 12, 55. Howson 92. Howson* 141.

DUBLIN, Ireland

Kilmainham Hospital.

This was completed between 1680 and 1684, built on the site of the Preceptory of the Knights Hospitaller and dedicated to the Martyr King Charles I. It includes a magnificent chapel with a moulded plaster ceiling. It ceased to function as an almshouse in 1928 and is now a National Centre for Culture and the Arts. The chapel is used for conferences, banquets and public functions.

Leaflet. Howson 108, 109, 118. Howson* 46–7. Doyle.

DURHAM

St Mary Magdalene Hospital.

The stone ruins of a medieval hospital chapel founded in 1449 are situated in

Magdalene Road off Gilesgate. Very little remains of the building, but a stone wall can still be seen at the rear of one of the houses which now occupy the area.

Website.

DUXFORD, Cambridgeshire

St John's Hospital.

The hospital was founded by Sir William de Coleville *c.*1200. It was used by the Knights Templar and Knights Hospitaller. The chapel is all that now remains of the hospital. It is a plain, very fine building. There is elegant moulding around the windows and decorative carving on the rood beam. In the south-east corner are a piscina and sedilia. The chapel continued to be used as a chantry after the hospital had fallen into disuse, but after the Reformation it was converted into a barn, the great east window being bricked up. The chapel has now been restored, and is administered by English Heritage.

Howson* 113–14. Website.

Above: Kilmainham Hospital, Dublin.

Below: The Hospital of the Holy Trinity, Croydon.

EAST GRINSTEAD, Sussex

Sackville College.

The college was founded by Robert Sackville, second Earl of Dorset, in 1609. The building was completed before 1622. By 1850 the chapel was in a very poor condition, and was restored in the Victorian style. The coved pentagonal roof was designed by William Butterfield *c*.1848. There are 18 stalls for the collegians and the Warden. The stained glass is also Victorian, including portraits of Pope Cornelius, the centurion kneeling before St Peter, St Susanna, the Blessed Virgin Mary and child. To the left of the centre window are four paintings on copper sheets depicting Sts Ermenild, Agnes, Katherine and Margaret. To the right of the window the paintings depict Sts John the Evangelist, Thomas Becket, Richard of Chichester and George. High on the south wall is a double quatrefoil opening to enable patients in the infirmary to hear the services. The door still has its original lock. The chapel also contains an alms-box, the old aumbry door with its Tudor carving, a rood cross, two 17th-century chests and a hutch to receive fines from the residents. The study of the Revd Dr John Mason Neale, one-time Warden, adjoins the chapel. It still contains the table at which he wrote 'Good King Wenceslas', and the window through which he looked out over the fields. Holy Communion is celebrated in the chapel regularly.

Chislett 14. Hallett 10, 55. Howson* 142.

EDINBURGH, Scotland

Magdalen Chapel.

This is a 16th-century almshouse chapel which after the Reformation became the Convening Hall for the Guild of

Above: Sackville College, East Grinstead.

Hammermen. A recent restoration has been commissioned by the Scottish Reformation Society.

Website.

ETON, Berkshire

Eton College.

The College and its chapel were originally founded in 1440 by King Henry VI as a school and hospital. There soon began to be difficulties in funding the almshouses, and they are thought to have been discontinued before the end of Henry VI's reign. By this time only the choir of the great pilgrimage church envisaged by King Henry had been built, and the 14 services each day which he had commanded were not accomplished. In 1479–82 Bishop Waynflete added an ante-chapel to produce the building we have today. Until the church was finished, services were held in the old parish church which was demolished in 1480. The wall paintings in what is now Eton College Chapel are in the Flemish style, dating from 1479–87. On the north side they depict miracles performed by the Blessed Virgin Mary. On the south side they tell the story of a medieval empress who was succoured by Mary. These were whitewashed over in 1560, rediscovered only in 1847, and restored as recently as 1957. All the glass in the chapel was destroyed by a bomb in 1940 with the exception of one window. The great east window by Eric Hone was installed in 1952. It depicts the Last Supper and the Crucifixion. The windows flanking it were designed by John Piper and executed by Patrick Reyntiens, depicting the miracles and parables of Jesus. The roof vaulting was constructed in medieval style in 1959, reflecting the original fan vaulting in Bishop Lupton's chapel of 1515.

Howson* 112. Goodman. Hatfield.

EWELME, Oxfordshire

God's House in Ewelme.

This charity was established in 1437 by William de la Pole, Duke of Suffolk and Alice, first Duchess of Suffolk and the granddaughter of the poet Geoffrey Chaucer. The almshouse chapel, dedicated to St John Baptist, is within the Parish Church of St Mary, at its southeastern corner. In the open timber roof of the chapel is a series of carved angels bearing shields. Six of these were replaced by modern replicas in 1937. The four lights of the east window contain fragments of stained glass, many of the pieces being contemporary with the church. The arms to be seen in the window include those of the Earl of Suffolk, of John of Gaunt, and of the Chaucers. The altar was designed by Sir John Ninian Comper in 1902. The figures in its reredos are St John Baptist, St Frideswide,

Left: God's House in Ewelme.

St Longinus, The Blessed Virgin with St John, St Birinus and St Michael. On the altar front are represented St George, St Sebastian and St Alban. The tiles on the sanctuary floor are some of those which originally covered the floor of the chapel. They show the fork-tailed lion of the Burgersh family and the wheel of the Roet family. The chapel also contains one of the ancient oak seats of the church and an old elm chest dating from around 1600. The fine tomb of Alice, Duchess of Suffolk (d.1475) lies within the chapel, as does the tomb of Thomas Chaucer (d.1434) and his wife Matilda Burgersh (d.1436).

Howson* 94–5. Guide book.

EXETER, Devon

St Catherine's Almshouses.

The remains of the chapel can still be seen. The almshouses were founded in 1457 and relocated in 1893. Subsequently the buildings were used as a shelter by the Church Army until they were destroyed in a bombing raid in 1942. A reconstructed inscription states that almspeople would be fined one penny if they did not remain at daily prayers from the beginning to the end.

Howson* 117. Website.

Above: St Catherine's Almshouses, Exeter.

E

Above and above right: Chapel exterior and interior, the Livery Dole Almshouses, Exeter.

The Livery Dole Almshouses.

These almshouses with their chapel were built in Heavitree between 1591 and 1594. The chapel of St Clare is distinct from the almshouses, being of red sandstone in contrast to the grey granite of the almshouses themselves. The chapel is surrounded by a garden, and a service is held there each Thursday.

Website.

Wynyards Almshouses.

These almshouses have an attached chapel in red sandstone, but it appears no longer to be in use.

Howson 117.*

Right and below: Wyatt Almshouses, Farncombe, Surrey.

St Anne's and St Francis' Almshouses.

These almshouses, founded in 1416, have a tiny chapel.

Howson 117.*

FARNCOMBE, Surrey

Wyatt Almshouses.

These were founded in 1622 and have a central gabled chapel. The will of the founder, Richard Wyatt, stipulated that 'everye Saboth daye if it be fayer weather goe all together to Godallmine Church to heare prayers there. If it be not fayer weather then one of them to say prayers in that Chappell or house which shalbe appointed for that purpose.' His widow Margaret Wyatt provided in her will of 1632 that a bible should be bought for the chapel. A number of commemorative boards have been placed in the chapel and include the Lord's Prayer and the Ten Commandments. There is also a brass tablet of Richard Wyatt, his wife and their six children kneeling either side of a table with open books, and a clock in black and gold colouring which is probably original to the chapel.

Website, Tancell.

F

FAVERSHAM, Kent

Faversham United Municipal Charities.

The present almshouses with their chapel were completed in 1863, replacing earlier almshouses which dated back to 1614. Their construction was made possible by a bequest from Henry Wreight. The architects were Hooker and Wheeler of Brenchley. The chapel is centrally situated so that residents can enter it through a covered way. Although the almshouses are built of brick, the chapel is built in Bath stone. It originally had two spires which became unsafe and were removed in 1964. The spires were restored on a slightly smaller scale in 1990 following a bequest by Peter Head. The design of the chapel resembles the apse of a late 13th-century or early 14th-century European cathedral. Its west end has since been enclosed to provide a residents' day room.

Many of the original furnishings remain – the pulpit, communion table and rails, and tiled panels in the apse. There are small chapels to the south and north, separated from the body of the building by traceried stone screens. The south chapel houses a fine Father Willis organ given in 1869 by the Giraud family. This was extensively restored by Martin Renshaw between 1978 and 2002. The five tall windows in the apse were installed in 1895 and depict New Testament scenes. The great west window, showing the Blessed Virgin and the Holy Child, Sts Peter and Paul, the arms of the Cinque Ports Confederation and the seals of the barons and town of Faversham, is the work of Thomas Willement. This was originally installed in Faversham Parish Church in 1844, and was brought to the almshouse chapel in 1911. A service is held in the chapel once a month, and concerts and organ recitals are frequently held there.

Shepherd.

FELBRIDGE, Sussex

Whittington College.

The college and its chapel were rebuilt away from their original site at Highgate in 1964–5. The chapel is integrated into the other buildings and services are held there each month.

Website.

FROLESWORTH, Leicestershire

Frolesworth Hospital.

The hospital was founded in 1656 and the present buildings date from 1725. The chapel is situated in the middle of the main walk from the entrance. It was

originally intended for the canonical use of members of the Church of England. The chapel has a handsome arched stone doorway with carved spandrels. It has quarried windows with stone mullions and a transom on which the words 'Blessed is he that considereth the poor' are carved. Above this is a stone turret with a clock. The interior is simple in arrangement, with rows of wooden benches.

Howson 127. Leaflet. Website. Hallett 36, 56.*

FROXFIELD, Wiltshire

Somerset Hospital.

The hospital was founded in 1686 under the will of Sarah, Duchess of Somerset, for the widows of clergy and estate workers. The chapel, completed in 1694, played a prominent part in the life of the hospital, or 'college'. A curate was appointed who received a salary of £10 per annum to read daily prayers, preach on Sundays and visit the sick. The widows were expected to attend Divine Service on Wednesdays and Fridays and twice on Sundays. The stipend was subsequently increased to £30 half yearly. The original chapel was built in the north-west corner of the quadrangle, but by 1813 this was so dilapidated that the Duchess' descendant, the Earl of Ailesbury, took responsibility for erecting the Gothic-style chapel sited in the centre of the quadrangle today. This is built of red brick with vitrified brick banding and a tiled roof, and an inscription recording its building is affixed to one of the side walls. The chapel windows have stained glass insets, one with the hatchment of the Duchess and the other with the coat

of arms of the Earl. The congregation at the College is still buoyant, with large attendances on special occasions such as Founder's Day. Two chaplains serve the College chapel at present.

Howson 144.*

GAMLINGAY, Bedfordshire

Sir John Jacobs' Almshouses.

The almshouses were built in 1665, but the chapel was not added until 1678. This date is etched in the glass of the chapel window. After it ceased to be used as a chapel, this building became a Sunday School. By 1981 it had become a scout hut. In 1995 the chapel was extensively restored and later occupied as an office by Gamlingay Parish Council. This arrangement ceased in 2012, when the Parish Council moved into new accommodation. The chapel has since undergone another restoration and awaits further use.

Website, Gorton.

GATESHEAD, Tyne & Wear

St Edmund's Hospital.

St Edmund's Parish Church, Gateshead, was originally the chapel of St Edmund's Hospital, founded in 1247 by Nicholas de Farnham, Bishop of Durham. His charter stipulates the appointment of a master and three priests to celebrate four masses every day. In 1448 the chapel passed into the hands of the nuns of St Bartholomew, Newcastle. Upon the Dissolution of the nunnery in 1540 the chapel passed into private hands and became a place of refuge for Roman Catholics. In 1549 it was the scene of the martyrdom of the Blessed John Ingram,

G

who had converted to the Church of Rome. By 1773 the chapel had fallen into a state of ruin, and was used as a builders' yard. In 1837 it was restored for worship, and in 1894, was incorporated into the new Holy Trinity Church. When Holy Trinity was declared redundant in 1969 the chapel of St Edmund was partitioned off and retained as a place of private prayer. In 1982 St Edmund's became the Parish Church of Gateshead. It is a simple, comfortable building decorated with brightly coloured banners.

Howson 22, 24. Howson* 142. Pl.4. Martin. Craig.

Trinity Almshouses.

The almshouses and their chapel were built in 1787.

Website.

GLASGOW, Scotland

St Nicholas' Hospital.

The hospital was established in 1456 by Bishop Andrew Muirhead and endowed with an income for the care of both laymen and priests. In 1789 the ruins of the hospital were acquired by the magistrates of Glasgow and were demolished with the exception of the building now known as Provand's Lordship, which was originally built as a manse for the chaplain of the hospital.

Hallett 12. Website.

GLASTONBURY, Somerset

The Magdalene Hospital.

The chapel of St Margaret is said to have been provided by St Margaret of Scotland to serve the hospital of St Mary Magdalene, which was founded in 1264. It has features dating from the 1200s and 1400s. One lancet window may be of a still earlier date. The

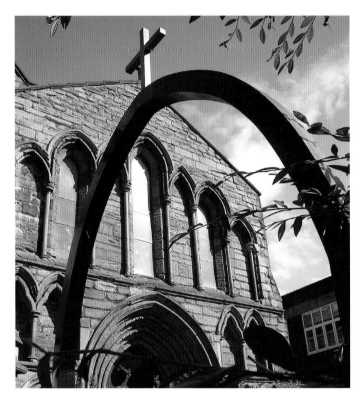

Above: St Edmund's Hospital, Gateshead.

present buildings were begun in the 1400s, and by 1610 were described as 'ancient'. The chapel was restored in the early 19th century and again in 1968. St Margaret is depicted in the bellcote. The building is now managed by the Friends of St Margaret's Chapel, and is open to all for prayer and meditation. Sufi meditation is held each Sunday evening.

Howson 81. Website.

St Patrick's Almshouses.

The almshouses were founded in 1517 and have long disappeared. Their chapel with its bellcote is currently being restored, and its medieval wall paintings depicting scenes from the life of St Patrick are newly exhibited.

Howson* 138. Website.

Right: St Margaret's Chapel, the Gloucester Charities' Trust.

GLOUCESTER

The Gloucester Charities' Trust.

St Margaret's Chapel was rebuilt in the early 1300s, incorporating a piscina and other parts of an earlier chapel possibly erected before 1100. It was restored in 1846 and 1875. The windows, a uniform set portraying apostles and Marys, are Victorian.

Leaflet. Hallett 8.

St Mary Magdalene's Chapel was a 13th-century Leper Chapel. The nave was demolished in 1861, but the chancel still stands. It shows interesting medieval graffiti. The name of St Mary Magdalene is continued by a group of almshouses elsewhere in the city.

Website.

St Bartholomew's Chapel is an early Gothic-revival building erected in 1789. It has now been converted into commercial premises, whilst its almshouses have relocated to another part of the city.

Howson[*] 120.

GODSTONE, Surrey

St Mary's Homes.

The houses, including their small chapel, were founded by Mrs. Augusta Nona Hunt and designed by Sir George Gilbert Scott in 1872.

Hallett 23, 56. Anderson. Website.

Right: St Mary's Homes, Godstone, Surrey.

GORING HEATH, Oxfordshire

The Goring Heath Almshouses.

These historic almshouses were founded in 1724 and the chapel was consecrated in 1742. The Grade One listed chapel is dedicated to St Bartholomew. It consists of a nave and chancel with a gallery. It is built of red brick in the Queen Anne style, and contains a three-decker pulpit and closed-in pews. There is a fine oak canopy over the entrance door. The chancel was built in 1799 and wainscoted with oak in 1808. A new chapel communion kneeler was created between 2003 and 2006 by the Royal School of Needlework, depicting the four seasons. A font has recently been presented, of Checkenden oak from Reed Estate, with a metal bowl. The chapel has recently been re-roofed.

Leaflet. History. Hallett 19. Howson* 135. Website.

GRAVESEND, Kent

Milton Hospital.

The Milton Chantry was the chantry chapel of the original leper hospital founded in 1322 by Aymer de Valence. Priests were employed there to say daily masses for the de Valence and Montechais families. The chantry was dissolved during the Reformation. Apart from the flinted east gable, the outside of the building has been bricked over. Remains of the 14th-century roof can be seen. A floor and chimney stack were inserted in the 16th century. The staircase with its decorated newel posts dates from the 17th century when the building became a tavern. The chapel now stands in a public park created in 1932 on the site of the New Tavern Fort. The

building is now a heritage and education centre under the care of English Heritage.

Howson* 124. Website. Anderson

GREATHAM, Cleveland

The Hospital of God.

The hospital and its chapel were founded in 1273 by Robert de Stichell, Bishop of Durham as The Hospital of God, St Mary and St Cuthbert. The charity was refounded in 1610 by King James I.

Howson* 38, 114. Website. Granath.

GREENWICH, London

Queen Elizabeth's College.

The college was originally erected in 1576 but was demolished and rebuilt in 1817–18. Nothing remains of the original buildings except for an oak joist on the west wall of the chapel which bears the following inscription, 'This old gurder taken out of the old chapel A.D.1576 Used by Thos. Bowen 1818'. A memorial window depicting William Lambard kneeling before Queen Elizabeth I was inaugurated by Queen Elizabeth II in 1974.

Guide Book.

G

Left and below: The Hospital of God, Greatham, Cleveland.

Opposite: The Goring Heath Almshouses, Oxfordshire.

Trinity Hospital.

This hospital was founded in 1613 by Henry Howard, Earl of Northampton. It was remodelled in the Gothic style in 1812. The small chapel has ancient coats of arms in its east window. The tomb and effigy of the Earl were transferred here some time after his death. Services are held weekly in the chapel.

Bold/Bradbeer/van derMerwe 43.

The Old Royal Naval College.

This building was founded in 1696 to the designs of Sir Christopher Wren and Nicholas Hawksmoor. It was originally the Royal Hospital for Seamen, a grand almshouse for former Royal Navy seamen who for reasons of age or disability were unable to maintain themselves. Occupation by the Greenwich Pensioners continued until 1869. In subsequent years the site was adapted for use as the Royal Naval College. At present it is the home of Greenwich University and Trinity College of Music. The original almshouse chapel was destroyed by fire in 1779. The present chapel, designed by James Stuart and William Newton, is a Neoclassical masterpiece. It is particularly noted for its plasterwork and castwork. The painter Benjamin West contributed the altarpiece, 'The Preservation of St Paul after Shipwreck on the Island of Malta' and designed four Coade stone statues of Faith, Hope, Charity and Meekness which are placed in the entrance vestibule. The organ was built by Samuel Green in 1787. The entrance door has a finely carved marble surround by John Bacon RA, flanked by monuments to Admirals Keats and Hardy, successive governors of the Hospital in the 1830s.

Behind the altar is a large monument to Sir John Franklin's lost Arctic expedition of 1845. The marble floor of the chapel is laid to a nautical cable pattern, and the pulpit is the top section of the original 'three-decker' which used to stand centrally. Services are held each Sunday in the chapel.

Bold/Bradbeer/van der Merwe 14. Hallett 56.

Below: Chapel interior, the Old Royal Naval College, Greenwich.

GUILDFORD, Surrey

Abbot's Hospital.

The hospital was founded as The Hospital of the Blessed Trinity by George Abbot, Archbishop of Canterbury, but has been known for most of its life by this honorific. The glass in the windows is attributed to the van Linge brothers, originally from East Frisia, who worked from London's south bank between the 1620s and the 1640s; it is dated 1621.

The stone window frames are thought to have been purchased from the former Dominican friary nearby, when its buildings were being dismantled and sold off in 1620. The glass tells the story of Jacob, perhaps as a compliment to King James I (Latin Jacobus) who awarded Abbot a charter to found the Hospital in 1622. The pews were brought from the old Holy Trinity Church after it fell down in 1740. A wooden post near the door contains a moneybox. The weekly Morning Service always includes a Prayer of Thanksgiving for Archbishop Abbot and his work. The original foundation stone has been brought inside and inserted into the wall behind the altar. It records G.A.+ and the date 1619.

Alexander 9-10, Taylor 22, 56, 63, 84. C.Benyon/ T.Benyon. Leaflet. Hallett 36, 57. Howson* 142. Richmond.

HACKNEY, London

Bishop Wood's Almshouses.

These almshouses were built in the 17th century in memory of Bishop Thomas Wood, Bishop of Lichfield. The small chapel at the north-east corner dates from a late 19th-century restoration. It is of red brick with stone dressings in a late 14th-century style. A service is held each week in the chapel.

Website.

HADLEIGH, Suffolk

Pykenham Almshouses.

These almshouses were founded by Archdeacon Pykenham in his will of 1497. The timber framed chapel, known as the

Above: Stained glass, Abbot's Hospital, Guildford.

H

Below: Pykenham Almshouses, Hadleigh, Suffolk.

Row Chapel and dedicated to the Blessed Mary Magdalene and St Catherine, stands in front of the almshouses. Following the rebuilding of the almshouses in 1887, the chapel was restored in 1890 by Dean and Mrs Spooner. The building features herring-bone brickwork and a tiled roof. Services are held in the chapel each Tuesday.
Howson* 140. Website.

HALIFAX, West Yorkshire
Joseph Crossley's Almshouses.
The almshouses were founded in 1863. The chapel, which is Congregational/URC, was originally large, but has been divided to provide meeting-room facilities. Several

busts of Joseph Crossley are to be found in the chapel, including one directly behind the minister's chair. The chapel possesses a fine French reed organ and a harmonium. An ecumenical service is held each Thursday.
Corry. Howson* 67.

HEMSWORTH, West Yorkshire
The Archbishop Holgate Hospital.
The hospital was originally founded by Archbishop Robert Holgate in 1555. Its present buildings are a Victorian replacement built around 1857. Services are held daily in the chapel, which is dedicated to the Holy Cross. The chapel was refurbished in 2000. The altar, in accordance

Left: Minister's chair and lectern, Joseph Crossley's Almshouses, Halifax.

with the medieval custom, has five legs. Jesus and the apostles are portrayed in the sanctuary arch. The roundels on the ceiling arches are 150 in number. The porcelain font, of Parian ware, is modelled on a stone font in Winchester Cathedral. The walls of the chapel bear the Stations of the Cross. The Sacrament is reserved in the Tabernacle. The altar cross and candlesticks were given in 1900 in memory of the wife of the then Master. The window above the altar was designed by Clayton & Bell and blessed in 1897. The stained glass windows portray the arms of Archbishop Holgate, his initials, St Peter, the Crucifixion, St Dorcas, Christ the King, the Good Samaritan, and the healing of the sick. The bell tower was rebuilt and the bell restored in 2003.

Vick 36–40. Vick in ACS 14–15. Corry.

HEREFORD, Herefordshire

The Coningsby Hospital.

Parts of the hall and chapel date from the 13th century when a house of the Knights of St John of Jerusalem was established. The almshouse was founded by Sir Thomas Coningsby in 1614. The chapel has a trussed rafter roof and contains a 13th-century coffin lid. The communion table of oak with eight legs in the form of Doric columns is early 17th century. In the north window are the arms of Coningsby (three coneys) impaling Fitzwilliam, dated 1614. The 17th-century pulpit is octagonal with carved panels. The plate includes a cup and cover paten of 1675 and an 18th-century pewter plate. On the west wall is a stone panel with the Coningsby arms and initials of 1597. A stained glass window depicting St John from Harewood Court was presented by Baron

Clive in 1981. The ante-chapel and upper floor now houses the Coningsby Museum.

Hallett 57. Beese 5. Howson* 40, 104.

St Giles' Hospital.

This was founded in 1290 for the use of the Friars Grisey, then became the property of the Knights Templar and later passed to the Crown. King Richard II donated it to the City of Hereford for use as an almshouse. The 12th-century round church was replaced by a building of 1682. This chapel originally stood on the corner of St Owen Street but was removed in 1927 and rebuilt next to the almshouses. Built into the west wall of the terrace is a large, much-worn stone carving depicting Christ in majesty. This is presumed to be part of the Romanesque tympanum of the original chapel. Services are held in the chapel weekly.

Website. Roderick.

William Price's Almshouses.

These almshouses are the bequest of William Price in 1604. The project was not completed until 1667. The almshouses contain ten dwellings, a chapel and a short wing at each end. The furnishings of the chapel are Victorian, and it possesses a French reed organ. Services are held monthly.

Leaflet. Roderick.

HEYTESBURY, Wiltshire

The Hospital of St John.

The hospital was originally founded in 1472 but was burnt down in 1765 and rebuilt in 1766–7. The complex includes a chapel. The original chapel was in the south-east corner of the Georgian building. The present chapel

was originally the coach house of the Custos where his horses were stabled and his coach kept. It was restored in 1962, the lower floor becoming a chapel with a flat above. The Custos was a clerk in holy orders from 1472 to 1990. At present the chapel is served by a team of chaplains.

Website. Richards.

Left and below: The Hospital of St John, Heytesbury, Wiltshire.

HIGHAM FERRERS, Northamptonshire

The Bede House.

This was founded by Archbishop Henry Chichele in 1423, replacing an earlier hospital of St James. Fragments of this are incorporated into the present building. The chapel opens from the eastern end of the hall. The walls are constructed of alternate courses of red and cream stone. The buildings fell into disrepair in the lare Middle Ages but were restored in the 1850s and are now used as a Sunday School.

Howson 41–3. Howson* 79, 81, Pl.6.

HULL, East Yorkshire

The Charterhouse.

The Carthusian Priory of St Michael was founded in 1378 by Michael de la Pole, first Earl of Suffolk. Within the priory stood a church for the brothers' use. An almshouse was established by the founder beside the lane between the river and the priory gate. The founder required the Master and almspeople to worship regularly together. A bull issued by Pope Boniface IX in 1394 granted permission for the establishment of two chapels in the almshouse. The almshouse buildings were damaged during

Below: Chapel interior, the Charterhouse, Hull.

H

H

Above: Portico, the Charterhouse, Hull.

the Civil War. When they were restored, the chapel was rebuilt in 1673 to the design of William Catlin. In 1675 the town's council gave £40 to provide a screen, pulpit, bell and seating. The bell is still in use, but the other furnishings were lost when the chapel was demolished and rebuilt by Master Bourne in 1777. The chapel now stands in the centre of the almshouse. In shape it is a parallellogram lit by a dome in the middle of the roof and by two plain glass windows, one in the east and one in the west wall. The ceiling is of plaster, flat and decorated with a delicate ornament in low relief. The floor, raised three steps high at the east end, is paved with squares of white stone with diamonds of slate at the angles. There are pews, a reading desk and a quaint semi-

circular pulpit in the north wall. Several mural tablets recall the names of successive Masters. The communion plate consists of a fine three-piece set made by John Langlands the Younger of Newcastle shortly after the building of the present chapel. The organ, made by the Hull firm of Forster and Andrews, was installed in 1902 and enlarged in the years following. It is now regarded as Hull's finest small organ. The chapel was significantly restored in 1981 under the supervision of Francis Johnson, architect, of Bridlington. Three handsome wooden chandeliers carved by Dick Reed of York, each embellished with an earl's coronet, were installed. The chapel stands at the centre of the House's life. Morning and Evening Prayer are read daily. The

Holy Communion is celebrated on Sundays and Wednesdays. Baptisms, weddings and funerals take place occasionally.

Corry. Deas. Howson 40.*

Hull United Charities.

By a scheme of 1887 several minor hospital and almshouse trusts in Hull were consolidated into the Hull Municipal Hospitals. A single large set of almshouses with a chapel was built to take the place of the former buildings. Further consolidations in 1913 and 1955 brought the existing Hull United Charities into being. The chapel is spacious and light, but is not often used for worship now.

Website.

Trinity House.

A chantry was established in Holy Trinity Church in 1456. The first chapel to be part of the Trinity House was built in 1461, and its chaplain was William Havington. This chapel was rebuilt in 1620. A new chapel was erected in 1772. In 1787 a gallery was added to accommodate boys from the newly formed school and additional residents and pensioners. The present chapel was completed in 1843, designed by H.F. Lockwood. The current chaplain is the 36th in succession.

Website. East.

Below: Façade, Trinity House, Hull.

HUNGERFORD, Berkshire

The Somerset Hospital.

The hospital was founded in 1686. It has a free-standing chapel in its courtyard.

Howson* 111.

HURST GREEN, Lancashire

The Shireburn Almshouses.

These were originally built in 1706 in Mitton, founded by Nicholas Shireburn and designed by John Mason. At the instigation of Fr Francis Vavasour SJ of Stonyhurst they were demolished stone by stone and rebuilt in the centre of the nearby village of Hurst Green in 1947. There is a three-bay pedimented range of two stories. The pediment has the arms of the Shireburns in lead in the tympanum, with two large supporting figures. There is lettering above the upper windows and fine foliage carving in the centre lintel. An imposing flight of steps leads to the former chapel, topped with urns, which stands between the two rows of almshouses.

Hallett 35. Howson 129. Howson* 57, Pl.19. Hartwell/N.Pevsner 2009: 349–50.

HURSTPIERPOINT, West Sussex

Almshouses of the Holy Name.

The almshouses designed by John Denman were founded in 1939. They are in a rather traditional 'tudorbethan' style with three cottages on either side of a small central chapel which seats nine. Inscribed memorial stones are placed on each side of the chapel door. The east window by Louis Ginnett depicts a young Christ figure. In the garden is a large stone surmounted by a crucifix.

Joyce.

Above: The Somerset Hospital, Hungerford.

Below: Almshouses of the Holy Name, Hurstpierpoint, West Sussex.

ILFORD, Essex

The Hospital Chapel of St Mary the Virgin & St Thomas of Canterbury.

This is the oldest building in the Borough of Redbridge. It was founded *c.*1145 by Abbess Adelicia of Barking as a hospice for infirm men. Barking Abbey, established in 666, was at that time a wealthy and influential

nunnery. The original dedication of the chapel was to St Mary the Virgin. When Mary Becket, sister of Thomas Becket of Canterbury, succeeded Adelicia as Abbess, she arranged for his name to be added. The chapel is in the centre of the almshouses. By 1219 the hospice was admitting lepers, and two chaplains served them in the chapel. The nave and chancel of the present chapel were built during the 14th century or earlier,

Below: The Hospital Chapel of St Mary the Virgin & St Thomas of Canterbury.

incorporating the original Norman wall as its north wall. An infilled window space was recently discovered in this Norman wall. The top of a painted mural can be seen there. A brass rubbing of Sir Jne Smith, master and chaplain, who died in 1475, has survived although the original brass disappeared from the chapel in the 18th century. Ilford Hospital Chapel survived the dissolution of Barking Abbey in 1539 because it had its own endowments and constitution, and continued as a chapel of ease as well as a hospice. The mastership was then leased out by the Crown. During the Civil War the hospital tithes were sequestrated and a plan was made to make the chapel into a parish church. But this was cancelled at the Restoration, after which the chapel passed through various hands until Bamber Gascoyne (1725–91) renovated it and provided new communion plate, still in the possession of the chapel. The final owner, Lord Salisbury, handed the hospice and chapel to the Diocese of Chelmsford who formed the Abbess Adelicia Charity to administer the site. The chapel is used for public events, and a service is held there each week.

Howson* 120. Website.

KENDAL, Cumbria

Sandes Hospital.
The courtyard and former chapel of the Hospital can be viewed from the gatehouse.
Hallett 57.

Sleddall Victoria Jubilee Almshouses.
These almshouses, built in 1887, also possess a former chapel.
Hallett 57.

KIRKLEATHAM, North Yorkshire

Sir William Turner's Hospital.

The hospital was founded in 1676. The chapel and the two school houses were remodelled in 1742 by Cholmley Turner, Sir William's great nephew. James Gibb, architect of St Martin in the Fields, is believed to have been responsible for the design of the chapel and for the acquisition of much of the furniture. The chapel has a stone façade, a clock tower, a cupola and dragon-shaped weather vane. Two life-sized statues of a boy and a girl stand high on the parapet. The interior of the chapel is designed in the Ionic style with a black and white Italian Carrara marble floor and Spanish mahogany pews. Above the entrance is a bridge with an exceptionally finely wrought iron balustrade, believed to be the work of Jean Tijou, and above the bridge is a finely sculptured bust of Sir William Turner. The centre panel of the window above the altar, depicting the adoration of the Magi, is a modified version of one of the ten windows designed by Francesco Sleter in 1721 for 'Cannons', the home of the Duke of Chandos. The panel and the adjacent side windows featuring Sir William as Lord Mayor of London and his elder brother John are exceptionally fine and rare examples of the work of William Price. The ceiling is arched in nine vaults. There are four Ionic columns made of wood and coated with sand to give the appearance of stone. The chapel also contains the death mask of Sir William Turner, a pair of candlesticks, a chandelier by the Dutch master craftsman Claude Demeny dated 1735, a silver mace and an altar cross. A full-length portrait of Sir William Turner is

Above: East window and altar, the chapel, Sir William Turner's Hospital, Kirkleatham.

a modern copy of a 17th-century work by Mary Beales.

Sotheran: 2001 9–14. Sotheran: 2008. Leaflet. Hallett 31, 58. Corry. Howson* 103, 114, Pl.16.

KIRKTHORPE, West Yorkshire

Frieston's Hospital.

The hospital, founded in 1595, is now used as a private dwelling. It has a central top-lit chapel.

Howson* pp.106–07, 150.

LANCASTER, Lancashire

Penny's Hospital.

The almshouses were built in 1715. Regular services are held in the chapel, which is very small with a bellcote and low shaped gables, uniform in design to the gateway, and bears the inscription 'Remember the congregation of thy poor'. The interior was remodelled in 1929–30. The panelling and furnishings are of oak.

Leaflet. Hartwell/Pevsner: 2009 393–4.

LEDBURY, Herefordshire

St Katherine's Hospital.

The hospital was founded by Bishop Hugh Foliot in 1232 and rebuilt in 1330. The old buildings were demolished and replaced in 1821 but the chapel – with its original tiled floor and impressive stained glass windows, provided as 'a constant reminder to all in the market place for the need for prayer and works of charity' – has been preserved. At present it is used by the Parish of Ledbury as a venue for midweek services of Holy Communion.

Hallett 6. Hillaby.

LEICESTER, Leicestershire

Wyggeston's Hospital.

The hospital was founded in 1513 as a religious community. Services in the chapel were a central part of the life of the hospital. Part of one wall of this building may still be seen in an area adjoining Leicester

Below: Chapel interior, Wyggeston's Hospital, Leicester.

and recently to the third. Fragments of stained glass from the first chapel, depicting St Ursula, an eagle and the Wyggeston arms, are exhibited in the present chapel, as are two panels of Victorian stained glass from the first chapel depicting the Presentation of Christ. These are believed to be by C.E. Kempe. The original dedication of the chapel was, 'the most glorious Virgin Mary, Mother of our Saviour, St Katharine and St Ursula and her fellows.' The present chapel is dedicated simply to St Ursula. The chapel now has a spacious and well-lit chancel and a shallow nave with gently angled seating. It possesses a small organ built in the 1960s by Henry Willis and two bells. Some interesting brasses and other memorials may be seen in the chancel. Services are regularly held in the chapel. In celebration of the Hospital's 500th anniversary a new Altar Frontal, created by Jackie Sibley and Jean Evans, was dedicated by the Bishop of Leicester on 6 January 2013.

Thawley 2, 3, 29, 35, 92, 93, plates 1–6.

Above and right: Victorian and modern stained glass at Wyggeston's Hospital.

Cathedral and Leicester Grammar School. When the hospital was reformed and new buildings were provided in 1867, a chapel was included in the scheme. The hospital was again rebuilt, complete with a new chapel in 1966. The silver-gilt chalice and paten of 1668 have been preserved, and are still used in the chapel. Memorials from the first chapel were transferred to the second,

Trinity Hospital.

In 1331 Henry Grosmont, 3rd Earl of Lancaster and Leicester, founded an almshouse in the Newarke, Leicester. His son, Henry, Duke of Lancaster, established a chantry college in 1354–6. In 1614 King James I granted a new Charter and gave the institution the name 'Hospital of the Holy Trinity'. The Chaplain was to be appointed by the Duchy of Lancaster. In 1994 the old hospital premises including the chapel were sold, and now constitute a section of De Montfort University. A new building on Western Boulevard was opened in 1995. The new chapel contained within these premises was consecrated by the Bishop of Leicester.

Howson* 127, Pl.5. Website.

LEWISHAM, London

Boone's Chapel.

Boone's Chapel was built in 1782 to serve a row of almshouses, and was mentioned by the diarist John Evelyn shortly afterwards as a pleasing building. The almshouses were demolished in 1877, after which the chapel was used as a reading room until it was brought back into use as a place of worship when the nearby church was bombed in World War II. It was last used in 1945 for a celebration VE Day service. The building, on Lee High Road, then became derelict but has recently been expertly restored to serve as an architect's office and showroom. The burial vault of the founder, Sir Christopher Boone, and his wife Mary, has been rediscovered. The chapel was attributed to Sir Christopher Wren but is now thought to be the work of his associate Robert Hooke. Some fine,

apparently original plasterwork remains around the window behind the altar. The exterior is in red brick with stone trim.

Binney 55. Howson* 130. Website.

The Almshouses' Chapel.

Following the demolition of the original Boone's Almshouses in 1877 a more extensive estate of new almshouses was erected in the neighbourhood of Lewisham, provided with a large chapel. These almshouses have in their turn been replaced, but the second chapel survives and is now incorporated into a Pentecostal Church.

Above and right: Boone's Chapel, Lewisham is still undergoing restoraton.

L

LICHFIELD, Staffordshire

The Hospital of St John Baptist Without the Barrs.

Bishop Roger de Clinton built a priory outside the gates (barrs) of the city of Lichfield in 1135 to serve pilgrims and travellers who arrived after curfew and were unable to gain entrance to the city. This was served by Augustinian Canons. The chapel was an integral part of these first buildings. In 1495 St John's was re-founded by Bishop William Smythe as a hospital for aged men, who were to be honest and devout and attend prayers every day. In the 17th century the chapel fell into ruins, but it had been restored and was once again in use by 1696. From 1716–21 the parishioners of St Mary's used the chapel while their own church was being rebuilt. They brought their own pews, which remained in the chapel afterwards, and had the chapel windows reglazed at their own expense. In 1829 an aisle was built on the north side, the former wall being replaced by a three-bay arcade. A gallery was installed in the aisle. There are several memorials to the Simpson family who were connected with the chapel for many years and had a family vault there. A stained glass window in the south is in their memory, and the Communion plate includes a silver flagon presented by Stephen Simpson in 1761. A thorough restoration was carried out in 1870. The walls of the nave were raised and the roof was more highly pitched. A magnificent stained glass window by John Piper representing Christ in Majesty and the Four Evangelists was installed in 1984. The Founders' Prayers are said in the chapel by the Master and Residents of the hospital each morning from Monday to Friday, and there are two celebrations of the Eucharist on Sunday mornings.

Clayton. Howson* 140.

Dr Milley's Hospital.

These almshouses were founded on property given by Bishop Heyworth in 1424. The hospital was re-endowed and rebuilt by Dr Thomas Milley, Archdeacon of Coventry and Canon of Lichfield, in 1502–04. The chapel is situated on the first floor of the building, above the entrance porch. It has a clear casement window, and a chest and cupboard dating back to the 16th century, as well as some ancient hassocks. The chapel was served until recently by the Sacrist and priest vicars of the Cathedral, but now has its own honorary chaplain. Services are occasionally held in the chapel, which has recently been redecorated, recarpeted, and supplied with new lighting.

Vinnicombe.

LINCOLN, Lincolnshire

St Anne's Bedehouses.

These were founded by Richard Waldo Sibthorpe and built to a design by A.W.N. Pugin. The chapel was built in 1854 by Charles Ward to a design by William Butterfield. The heart of the founder is reputedly buried in the chancel. The organ was moved to the chapel from the nearby hospital which was bombed during the Second World War. The chapel is detached from the main building and has its own graveyard. Services are held fortnightly, but these are no longer compulsory as was the original instruction of the founder.

Crust 49, 60–1, 69. Howson 147, 156. Brochure. Howson* p.67.

LINGFIELD, East Sussex

The College of St Barnabas.

The college was founded in 1895. The earliest section of its main chapel was dedicated by the Bishop of Rochester in 1902. It was completed to a design by John Oldrid Scott & Sons in 1909. The altar and reredos are by A.L. Moore. 84 bosses of individual designs are carved in the panelling behind the stalls. There is also carving along the front of the stalls, the altar rails and the ends of the pews. The seating is arranged in collegiate fashion. At the east end are two statues of the Blessed Virgin Mary, one of St James and one of St John. A plaque depicts St Barnabas. The reredos shows the Christus Rex, Moses and Elijah. The restoration of the Pre-Raphaelite panels by Francis Ashton Jackson on the gallery screen has been revealed as some of his best work. The pictures in the chapel are copies of originals by Titian, Reni, Dolci and Raphael. The east window by C.E. Kempe was dedicated in 1906. Its subject is *Urbs Beata*, the New Jerusalem built upon the foundation of the apostles and prophets. A series of scrolls contains verses of a hymn by St Bernard of Cluny, four in the original Latin and ten in English translation by J.M. Neale. The remaining windows, by F.C. Eden, portray the Eastern and Western doctors of the Church. On the exterior of the chapel are statues by Bridgeman of Christ and St Barnabas.

There is also a smaller chapel on the ground floor, built originally as a mortuary chapel in 1928. This is furnished in a simple, modern style. It has a small set of Stations of the Cross from Italy.

Guide Book. Peel. Website. Such.

LINLITHGOW, West Lothian

St Mary's Chapel.

An almshouse was founded in Linlithgow as a result of a grant by Henry de Levingston in 1496. The hospital and the chapel of the Blessed Virgin Mary formed part of what was then known as the Middleraw. The chapel and hospital were still in existence in 1553. The site was last excavated in 1982, when no trace of the chapel could be found.

Website.

LINTON-IN-CRAVEN, North Yorkshire

Fountaine's Hospital.

This hospital, founded in 1721 by Richard Fountaine, is thought to have been designed by Sir John Vanburgh or his associate Nicholas Hawksmoor. The buildings are on a grand scale, in the

L

Below: A summer event at Fountaine's Hospital, Linton-in-Craven, North Yorkshire.

Palladian style. Sir Richard's will specified that his almshouses should have 'a chapel in their midst, that the almspeople must attend whenever prayers were said in it' and 'to pay the Rector of Linton, as long as he resides in the parish and says prayers twice a week'. The chapel with its tower and cupola is at their centre. The round-headed doorway of the chapel has massive pilasters on each side, going up to the parapet. The kneelers and altar cloth were made by local craftsmen. Morning Prayer is said each Tuesday, and Holy Communion and Evensong are held once a month.

Corry. Howson 129, 131. Howson* 56, 147. Leaflet.

LLANGEVIEW, Monmouthshire

The Roger Edwards Charity.

Services were regularly held in the chapel until the 1980s, when it was converted into an almshouse. The ecclesiastical windows remain.

LLANRWST, Conwy

The Gwydir Amshouses.

These were founded in 1610 by Sir John Wynne of Gwydir and closed in 1976. The adjacent chapel is at the south-east corner of Llanrwst Parish Church. A tablet installed by Richard Wynne records the building of the chapel in 1633. It is said that Inigo Jones, a friend of Sir Richard, assisted in its design. It originally opened into the church but was later closed off by panelling. The chapel now contains part of Llewelyn the Great's stone coffin, as well as other remnants of local heroes.

Hart 54, 64, 66, 144, 153, 159. Leaflet.

LONDON

The Charterhouse.

The Charterhouse derives its name from the Carthusian priory that stood on the site from 1371 until the Dissolution. The almshouse of Sutton's Hospital in Charterhouse occupies buildings which were originally an aristocratic mansion before being adapted in the early 17th century as an almshouse and school. The school moved elsewhere in 1872. A chapel built in 1349 became the Carthusian priory church and was demolished in 1545. The wall lines of

Below: Chapel interior, the Charterhouse, London.

this church have been excavated and can still be seen. The south aisle of the present chapel was the chapterhouse of the priory, consecrated in 1414 and rebuilt *c*.1512. The north aisle was added by Francis Carter in 1613–14, as was the Chapel Cloister to connect the chapel to the Master's Court buildings. Between the two aisles he built a splendid Tuscan colonnade. The chapel was further extended in 1825 when a large bay was added on the north side of Carter's aisle. The chapel was restored by Edward Blore in 1843, when a font of Caen stone was installed, part of the tower demolished, and the present ceilings created. The aisle was realigned and a carved wooden screen placed beneath the arch. The pulpit and communion table are Jacobean. The panelling in the sanctuary, originally by Blore, was modified in the 1880s ; behind it is a piscina. Above the communion table hangs an oil painting by Giordano depicting the Visitation of the Blessed Virgin Mary to Elizabeth. The east window, by Charles Clutterbuck in 1844, depicts the Crucifixion. The tomb of Thomas Sutton was transferred to the chapel in 1614. A gallery was installed by Blore to house the Walker organ of 1841. Services are held in the chapel daily. When a new medical wing was added to the hospital, a small fully accessible chapel was incorporated, dedicated to St Bruno, and was dedicated by the Bishop of London on 23 June 2004.

Porter/Richardson 2000: 26–32. Howson 88, 95. Howson* 39, 99.

Below and right: Trinity Almshouses, Mile End.

St Martin-in-the-Fields Almshouses.

These were founded in Charing Cross and were relocated in 1618 to the Charing Cross Road. They later moved to Camden Town in 1818. The chapel at the rear of the buildings has since been converted into almshouses.

Howson* 65, 129. Website.

The Savoy Chapel.

The walls of the current chapel incorporate part of an earlier chapel from the great hospital or almshouse founded nearby by Henry VII in 1512. These original buildings were magnificent, and contained three chapels. In 1702 this hospital was dissolved, and the buildings were used for other purposes. They were demolished in the 19th century with the exception of the hospital's main chapel, dedicated to St John Baptist. After fires in the mid-19th century gutted the chapel it was rebuilt and restored in 1865. The Savoy Chapel is now a private chapel of the sovereign in right of the Duchy of Lancaster. It is also the chapel of the Royal Victorian Order. Extensive restoration in 2000 restored the ceiling to its earlier glory.

Porter/ Richardson. Howson* 91, 132.

Trinity Almshouses, Mile End.

The hospital was built in 1695 by the Corporation of Trinity House on land bequeathed to it by Captain Henry Mudd of Ratcliff in the style and period of Sir Christopher Wren. By 1696, 28 houses

L

Above: Almspeople at St Peter's Hospital, c.1860

Below: St Peter's Hospital, Wandsworth Common, after 1850: 19th-century illustration.

and a chapel had been built. The chapel is set prominently at the far end of the main court. The original floor level has been lowered following the fall of one of the ancient pensioners down the steps. The exterior of the building is covered with cement and lined over to represent stone. It has a clock, turret and weather vane, and there are carved wood brackets and cornices. The roof has green slates. The stained glass windows in the southeast and southwest depict the arms of Wardens and Masters including the Duke of Wellington and Duke of Clarence. An inscription in the southeast window records its removal from the Trinity Hall at Deptford in 1786 and its being placed in the chapel in 1793. The stained glass window panes are now on display in the library of the historic Trinity House headquarters, EC3N.

Ashbee. Hallett 21. Howson 112, 113, 123. Howson* 52, 106-07, 131. Jones.

Vintners' Almshouses.

A survey of 1722 states that prayers were offered in this chapel on Sundays, Wednesdays, Fridays and Holy Days.

Website.

St Peter's Hospital.

These almshouses were founded by the Fishmongers' Company at Newington Butts in 1618. They included a chapel. The almshouses were rebuilt in 1850 on Wandsworth Common.

Website.

LONG PRESTON, North Yorkshire

The Hospital of James Knowles.

The large chapel of the hospital, founded in 1613, has been converted into an almshouse.

Corry. Howson* 147.

LUDLOW, Shropshire

The Hospital of the Holy Trinity, the Virgin Mary, and St John Baptist..

This hospital stood at the northern end of the Teme Bridge and was founded in the 1220s by the Ludlow Burgess Peter Undergod. The hospital church was built at or shortly after its foundation, and the hospital's right to celebrate divine service there was confirmed by the patron before 1241. The endowment of a daily mass in the hospital church by Richard of Eastham is recorded in 1364. An indulgence for the repair of the hospital's bells was obtained in 1411. By the 15th century the hospital seems to have developed into a small college of priests whose principal functions were to serve chantries and obits in the hospital church. In 1535 the hospital contained a master and two chaplains, both of whom had been there for over 20 years. Conventual life at the hospital had ceased by 1546. Part of the hospital buildings were converted into a house, but the church was still being used for worship, presumably as a private chapel, in 1564 when Jane, widow of William Foxe, left a chalice and other church goods there to her son Edward. It was apparently intact in 1577, when a sketch shows a small rectangular building with a round-headed door on its northwest gable, two round-headed windows on the southwest wall, and a bellcote near the southeast gable. The church was described as 'decayed' in 1593 and was largely demolished by Ludlow corporation in 1636, when the materials were used to repair the parish churchyard wall. Only the tall pointed arch of the church now remains.

Howson* 137. Gaydon/Pugh 102–04.

Foxe's Almshouses.

Shortly before his death in 1590 Charles Foxe began to erect four almshouses near St Leonard's Chapel which had once belonged to the Knight's Hospitaller of Dinmore. The almshouses were completed after his death, and were administered by the Foxe family until 1769. In this year James Foxe assigned the almshouses and St Leonard's Chapel to the corporation of Ludlow on the understanding that they would repair the chapel. The corporation kept the almshouses in good repair, but did not honour their agreement to repair the chapel. In 1787, being in a dangerous condition, it was illegally demolished and the stone used to build a bridge over the river Corve. Responsibility for the almshouses passed

L

from the corporation to a board of trustees in 1863. A separate fund for rebuilding St Leonard's Chapel was set up. Sir G. Gilbert Scott was commissioned to design it, and in 1870 the new chapel was built.

Watts 64–6. Pevsner 2002: 186.

MAIDSTONE, Kent

The Boniface Hospital.

Only the gateway and chapel remain of this hospital, founded in 1260 by Boniface, Archbishop of Canterbury and re-founded in 1395 by Pope Boniface IX. The chapel, built in 1395, originally served as a chantry, and was suppressed in the first year of King Edward VI. It is now the Parish Church of St Peter.

Howson* 125. Page 232–3. Website.

MALDON, Essex

St Giles' Hospital.

This was originally a leper hospital founded by Henry II. In 1481 it was granted by Edward IV to Beeleigh Abbey. When the Abbey was dissolved, the hospital was also closed and became part of a barn. The remains of the hospital, including its 12th-century chapel, were again revealed when the barn was pulled down in 1913.

Howson* 120. Website.

MALMESBURY, Wiltshire

St John's Almshouse.

The almshouse stands, with the Court House, on the site of the medieval hospital of St John. Its chapel is said to have been built at the gift of King Athelstan, in honour of God and St John Baptist. In 1265 a judgment of the Bishop of Salisbury is recorded which declares that only the

Prior and Brothers and Sisters wearing the habit and badge of the Order may hear and receive Divine Office in the chapel of the hospital. All that remains of the chapel today is an arch facing the road, which must have formed the west door, surmounted by a smaller arch, which would have been a window. These transitional or very early English arches date the chapel to the late 12th century or early 13th. The chapel was structurally connected with the other almshouse buildings. A 1623 reference shows that, although the religious community had been replaced by an almshouse maintained by the Alderman and Burgesses, the chapel was still in use. The almshouse is presently in bad repair, and there are plans to convert it into a museum.

Website.

MARGATE, Kent

Michael Yoakley's Charity.

The charity was founded by Michael Yoakley, one of the first Quakers, in 1709. In *c.*1750 the cottage adjacent to the Clock House was converted into a Quaker Meeting House. Today non-denominational services and Quaker meetings are held there.

Leaflet.

MARSHFIELD, South Gloucestershire

The Crispe Almshouses.

These almshouses were built by Nicholas Crispe, a member of the Skinners' Company, and Ellis Crispe, who was probably a member of the Salters' Company, between 1612 and 1619. The cottages have a central chapel. The coats of arms on the stone tablet in the chapel are of the Skinners' and Salters' Companies of which the Crispe brothers were members. A monthly service of Holy Communion is still held in the chapel. The building has a small spire above and a porch attached to the front.

Website. Colbourne.

MELBOURNE, Derbyshire

Thomas Cook's Memorial Trust.

The almshouses are served by the Thomas Cook Memorial Hall. This is furnished as a Baptist Chapel, Thomas Cook having been a fervent Baptist. It has a dais at one end with brass rails. It is now mainly used as a community hall, but a religious and social meeting for the elderly named 'The Friendly Hour' takes place on Thursdays.

Leaflet.

NEWARK, Nottinghamshire

The Bede House.

This tiny stone chapel of 1558 is the sole surviving building of a group of almshouses founded by William Phillipot. The chapel is of local limestone with a stone slate roof and wooden bell turret at one end. The recessed door is protected by a carved stone arch.

Howson 134. Website.*

NEWCASTLE UPON TYNE.
Tyne & Wear

Holy Jesus Hospital.

This hospital is one of only two surviving 17th-century brick buildings in the city. The site contains the remains of a 14th-century sacristy wall, part of the church wall and a window from an Augustinian friary. The friary was dissolved in 1539,

after which the friary buildings were used for meetings of the Council of the North. The Holy Jesus Hospital occupied the site from 1682, worshipping at the nearby All Hallows Church, until the residents were moved to the St Mary Magdalene Charity north of Newcastle in 1937. The Holy Jesus buildings are now administered by the National Trust.

Howson Pl.17. Leaflet. Redhead.*

Trinity House.

The seafarers in the area had formed themselves into a fraternity some time after 1335, and in 1505 the present site was purchased. The order to commence the building of the chapel was made in the same year. The brethren also leased pews and maintained an altar within the

Below: Pews and panelling in Trinity House chapel, Newcastle upon Tyne.

N

old All Hallows' Church. The interior panelling was added in 1634, and 53 cherubs were carved in 1635 followed by a further four in 1636. The roof was renewed in 1651. A bell in the roof dating from 1685 bears the inscription, 'If God is with us, who is against us?' The Bead-folk who occupied the almshouses followed a regular tradition of praying for the souls of their benefactors. The chapel is still in regular use today. A special service is held on Trinity Sunday and a Remembrance Service in November. Christenings are performed in an upturned bell, draped around with a flag. The three panels of stained glass were provided by the Henzel family between 1911 and 1930. The same family presented the organ in 1917. The chapel contains numerous commemorative plaques, and nine colours have been laid up there. The altar was brought down from All Sts' Church to Trinity House in 1550. Several old Bibles and Books of Common Prayer used by former Masters and embossed with the names of their owners are preserved in the chapel.

Guide Book 35–37. Howson* 142.

The Hospital of St Mary.

A single pillar provides a plaque recording that this once marked the entrance to Newcastle Grammar School, which was built on the foundations of the former chapel of the medieval Hospital of St Mary.

NEWINGTON BUTTS, London

Drapers' Almshouses .

These almshouses were founded by John Walter in 1650. A chapel was erected alongside the eight original almshouses.

The almshouses were rebuilt about 1778, recast in 1888 and demolished in 1961.

Website. Fussell.

NEWLAND, Worcestershire

Beauchamp Almshouses.

The Church of St Leonard, built in 1861–64, is connected by a cloister to the almshouses which stand on the other three sides. The square-vaulted lower stage of the steeple serves as a lobby for the almspeople. The interior is elaborate, with wall paintings and rich stained glass. A four-bay arcade between chancel and aisle is early French Gothic in style with alternate pairs of light and dark columns. This separated the female pensioners in the aisle from the men who sat behind the choir stalls. In the west wall of the nave a romantic canted oriel, gabled as if it were part of a castle, connects with the infirmary on the upper floor of the adjoining matron's house. The reredos was original to the church and was carved by Boulton's of Cheltenham in white Caen stone. The figures of Christ's crucifixion were painted in 1928. The cylindrical font, originally from the church of St Thomas adjoining Great Malvern Priory, dates from *c.*1200. The lychgate is built of timber from the 14th-century church. A small chapel can be found in the eastern side of the east range of the almshouses. This was built as a mortuary in 1865, using timbers from the 14th-century church. It has trefoiled stained glass windows. The site of the original church, also dedicated to St Leonard, is a little to the south. The site of the altar is marked by a large cross. From the consecration of the church until 1945 there was a choir school known as Newland Choir

Right: Church of St Leonard, Beauchamp Almshouses, Newland, Worcestershire.

N

Above: Huggens College, Northfleet, Kent, as seen in *The Illustrated London News*, c.1870.

Right: Huggens College, from an old postcard.

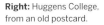

School' where the choristers boarded and sang daily services in the church.

Website. Brownlee.

NORTHAMPTON, Northamptonshire

The Hospital of St John the Baptist and St John Evangelist.

According to Leland the hospital was founded by William Sancte Clere, the Archdeacon of Northampton, whose name first occurs in 1144. In 1330 William de Horkesle and Emma his wife obtained a licence to grant a messuage payable to the master and brethren of the hospital of St John to find a chaplain to celebrate daily in the chapel of the said hospital for the souls of the faithful departed. A chantry for the souls of William and Emma was formally ordained in the church by the Bishop of Lincoln in 1339. In 1340 another chantry for the soul of John de Duglington was ordained at an altar on the west side of the lady chapel next to the organs. The church, rebuilt in 1309, seems to have been one of considerable size for an institution of this kind. In 1310 a licence was issued for the dedication of four altars there. In 1433 Bishop Gray dispensed the brethren from finding a secular priest as their funds were impoverished, and licensed one of the brethren to officiate in his place. The master's house and garden, together with the chapel, were sold in 1870 to the Bedford and Northampton Railway Company by whom the chapel was sold to Mr Mullinger, who transferred it to the use of the Roman Catholic congregation. It is situated to the east of the main buildings.

Howson 22, 44, 45, 50. Howson* 86, 88, 133. Serjeantson/ Adkins 156–159. Website.

NORTHFLEET, Kent

Huggens College.

This almshouse charity was established in 1847 by John Huggens. The orginal chapel was built in 1870. The 19th-century buildings, including the chapel, were demolished in 1968, and new bungalows and a chapel were built on part of the site. The new chapel was soon found to be too small, and with the aid of a generous legacy the east end was extended and the chapel was dedicated in 1973 to St John the Evangelist. The north wall windows contain coats of arms of several of the Trustees. A stained glass east window by Bronwen Gordon was dedicated in 1978. The furniture in the Sanctuary and the organ are from the demolished Victorian chapel. The chapel was refurbished with new lighting in 2011.

Website. Hunnisett.

NORWICH, Norfolk

The Great Hospital.

The Great Hospital was founded in 1249. The church of St Helen, Bishopsgate, was rebuilt within the hospital site between 1270 and 1400. Its west end was rebuilt as an infirmary and to the east was a large chancel whose ceiling was decorated with at least 252 panels, each depicting a black eagle. At the Reformation both were walled off and converted into ward accommodation. This left an almost square-shaped church with a very high roof. It has a central pulpit of the 18th century surrounded by box pews, and the altar is in the Lady Chapel to the south. The altar is from the 15th century. The bosses in the vaulted roof of the Lady Chapel represent a sculptured hymn of praise to

Above: The 1970s extension to the east end of the chapel, Huggens College.

the Virgin Mary. The Creed Board behind the altar is early Georgian. A copy of 'The Transfiguration' by Raphael is behind the pulpit. The silver sanctuary lamp is *c.*300 years old. The benches on either side of the two front pews are outstanding examples of medieval wood carving made between 1519 and 1532, depicting SS Margaret, Luke, Matthew and Mark. The stained glass window of St Helen is believed to be of the early 20th century. A small glass panel of St Giles, patron of the hospital, was made locally and presented in 1991. The church continues to serve the hospital and a small parish congregation.

Phillips. Terry/Youngs. Howson 87, 88, 132.*

OAKHAM, Rutland

The Hospital of St John and St Anne.
The chapel of St John was built 1300–20,
predating the hospital which was founded by
William Dalby in 1399. The pointed doorways
in the north, west and east walls date from 1300.
The walls were largely rebuilt or heightened
in the late 14th century or early 15th century.
The roof and parapet is of the 15th century.
On the outside may be seen grotesque heads at
parapet level and a stone sundial. The hospital
fell into disrepair and was refounded by a
Royal Charter granted to Archdeacon Robert
Johnson in 1597. The original buildings were
demolished to make room for the railway in
1845, whilst the chapel was spared, restored in
1858 and brought back into use in 1865. The
chapel was restored again in 1912/13. At this
time it was used intermittently, and during
the Second World War it was a repository for
the storage of furniture from war-damaged
houses. In 1949 it was taken over by the Parish
of Oakham as a Church Hall and occasional
worship centre, officially becoming a Chapel of
Ease in 1955. In 1983 almshouses were again
erected adjacent to the ancient chapel, which
was re-consecrated to its original purpose by the
Bishop of Peterborough following a complete re-
ordering. A chalice donated in 1821 by the Revd
George Osbourne is now kept at Oakham Parish
Church. The Royal Charter was supplemented
by HM Queen Elizabeth II in 1997, and the
Supplemental Charter hangs on the South Wall
of the chapel. Extensive repairs were carried out
in 2009 to ensure the integrity of the structure.
Services are regularly held in the chapel.
Matthew. Website.

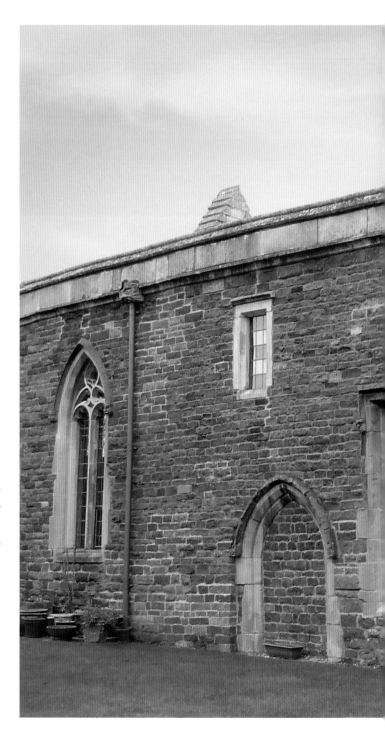

Right: The Hospital of St John and St Anne,
Oakham, Rutland.

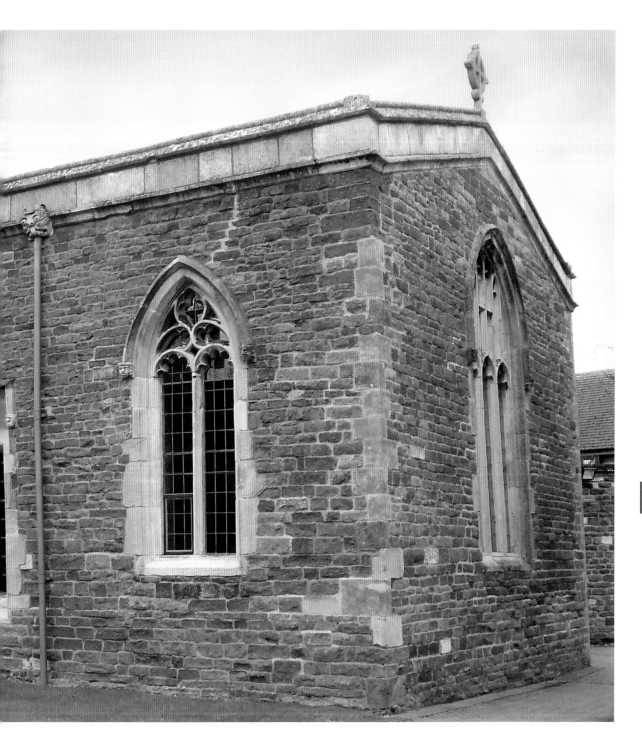

OSPRINGE, Kent

The Hospital of St Mary.

A significant fragment remains of the medieval hospital and hostel for kings built early in the 13th century along Watling Street. Until the foundation was dissolved on the instructions of King Henry VIII, the Maison Dieu was a considerable landmark along the pilgrim route and for travellers to Canterbury, Dover and the Continent. Rebuilt on stone foundations in the 16th century, two buildings remain. St Mary's is now a private residence. The Maison Dieu opened as a village museum in 1925.

Website.

POPLAR, London

The East India Company's Almshouses.

The almshouses with their chapel were opened in 1628. Disorder in the house in 1635 led to the introduction of regulations and the reading of prayers by one of the pensioners in the chapel. The chapel

assumed a greater influence and for a time was the main centre of worship in Poplar. It became a school in 1657. Additional almshouses were built in 1798–99, and the original almshouses were demolished and replaced in 1801–02. Expansion continued until 1866 when the almshouses, excluding the chapel, burial ground and chaplain's house, were sold and soon demolished. The chapel then became the Parish Church of St Matthias, which closed in 1976.

Hobhouse 107–110. Website.

PRESTON ON THE WEALDMOOR, Shropshire

Preston Hospital.

The hospital, originally consisting of almshouses for women and a school for girls, was founded in 1716 by Catherine, Lady Herbert. The buildings were completed in 1726. Their architect was Francis Smith of Warwick. The almshouses are built on three sides of a quadrangle with a hall in the centre of the north wing, slightly higher than the rest of the building and crowned by a square lantern with a clock. The hall has giant pilasters, two large arched windows and a grand doorway. The interior panelling is contemporary. It was used as the schoolroom and, on Sundays, as the chapel. The buildings were sold in 2002–03 and replaced by purpose-built almshouses in Newport.

Watts 90–5. Pevsner 2002: 232.

PUTNEY, London

Licensed Victuallers' Benevolent Institute.

These cottages were founded in 1827 and built in 1828. They have a monumental stucco chapel with a pediment and belfry.

Website.

Left: The Church of St Matthias, Poplar.

O

RERECROSS, North Yorkshire

Rerecross Hospital or The Spital on Stainmoor.
The hospital was given *c.*1171 by Ralph de Multon as a shelter for travellers across the wild moorland track leading from Yorkshire to Westmoreland. It was served by the nuns of Marrick, who paid a stipend to the chaplain. Tithes and offerings in the chapel were to be paid to the Hospital of St Peter at York.
Website.

RICHMOND, North Yorkshire

Bowes Hospital.
The almshouse was placed inside the small church of St Edmund, built in 1607. It has been converted into a private house, but the buttresses and a window of two lights remain, as do two short lengths of plaster frieze.
Howson* 147. Pevsner 1966: 299.

The Hospital of St Nicholas.
The hospital was in existence by 1172. Originally its priest celebrated Mass at the Chapel of St Edmund elsewhere in the town, but by 1448 a chantry had been built at the hospital. In 1546 Mass was said on three days each week at the hospital and three days at St Edmund. The chapel has since been converted into a house.
Page 1974: 321–330. Pevsner 1966: 299.

RIPON, North Yorkshire

The Hospital of St Mary Magdalen.
The chapel formed part of a leper hospital founded by Archbishop Thurstan in 1115. It was the duty of the Sisters to maintain a priest to celebrate Mass in the chapel. The 'low side' or 'leper' window may have served as a means of communication between the lepers and the chapel. In the 14th century leprosy had declined, so that the hospital became a lodging for the sick and destitute. Two abbots of Fountains, Marmaduke Huby (1439–1526) and Marmaduke Bradley (1485–1555) were Masters of the hospital. The almshouses were rebuilt in 1674 and again restored in 1875. The Deans of Ripon have been Masters of the hospital since 1688 and have appointed chaplains to serve the chapel. The shape of the chapel is unchanged from its 12th-century foundation. It has a Norman font and doorway, a 15th-century oak screen, and finely carved oak pews. The east window is Perpendicular, a later addition to the building, but containing ironwork and glass fragments of medieval origin. The ancient Norman stone altar survives. The marble tesserae in the floor of the sanctuary may have been brought from the ruins of a Roman villa. The remains of a wooden bell are preserved, possibly recalling the custom of replacing the metal bell with a wooden one in Lent. The former leper chapel was abandoned in 1858 but was restored and brought back into general use in 1989.
Corry. Hallett 8. Howson 21, 22, 24. G.T. Jones. Barber. Howson* 23, 147.

The Hospital of St Anne.
This was originally founded early in the 12th century or possibly in 1438. The ruins of this chapel may still be seen. Later it gave its name to the Victorian Chapel of St Anne, built in 1858 to replace the former leper chapel. When the leper chapel was reinstated for general worship in 1989, St Anne's Chapel was sold as a private house.
Corry. Howson 25. Howson* 23, 25, 147.

R

Left: The ruins of St Anne's Chapel, Ripon.

The Hospital of St John Baptist.
This was founded by Archbishop Thomas II in 1109. An Inquisition in 1341 reported that there was a dedicated chapel, and recommended that a chaplain be found for it. In 1454 Archbishop William Booth granted 40 days' indulgence to all who visited the chapel on certain days, or who gave of their goods to the chapel. The *Valor Ecclesiasticus* in 1535 recorded that Mass and other divine services were regularly celebrated. The chapel ceased to be used for worship in 1722 and the building had various uses, including a school, until it was restored and rededicated in 1858. It is still regularly used for worship by the residents of the surrounding almshouses.
Howson* 23, 147.

ROCHESTER, Kent
The French Hospital : La Providence.
The hospital was founded in 1718 for poor and infirm Huguenot refugees and their descendants. In 1865 it moved from Finsbury to a new building at Hackney which included a chapel . The hospital relocated to Horsham after the war, and again to Rochester in 1960. The present building has no chapel, but it employs a chaplain who holds a service of Holy Communion each week in a suitably furnished common room with a 17th-century stained glass window.
Brown.

SAFFRON WALDEN, Essex
King Edward VI Almshouses.
The almshouses were originally founded in 1400 by the Guild of Our Lady of Pity. The original almshouses were timber-framed, with a large chapel at the centre.The Guild was dissolved at the Reformation, but on the petition of Sir Thomas Smith, King Edward VI granted letters patent for the founding of

R

the King Edward VI almshouses of Walden. The 15 almspeople were required to attend services three times a day. When William Cole visited the almshouses in 1770 he wrote: 'In the ordinary chapel of the Almshouse hangs a brass sconce near the desk, where prayers and a sermon are occasionally read, by a layman, to the poor inmates. In the side window of the chapel is the half-figure of a monk, in blue. In another window are three or four pieces of old painted glass, one a head of our Saviour, a second of our Lady, and the third of a bishop, mitred. In the same window is a neat, modern coat of arms.' Henry Harrison, the local architect, drew up plans for a long two-storey building with a central chapel, rather on the lines of an Oxbridge college, in 1828. This chapel remains, with its coat of arms, high vaulted ceiling and leaded windows. It is not used for worship at present, but serves as a common room and meeting room. A silver mazer bowl, dated 1507–08 and having at its centre a figure of the Virgin and Child, probably belonged to the original chapel. Samuel Pepys drank from it in 1660. It is now in the British Museum.

Brooker/Whiteman. Everett/Stewart. Cooper. Collingwood.

SALISBURY, Wiltshire

St Nicholas' Hospital.

The earliest reference to the hospital is in 1215, when ten acres of land are recorded as having been donated to it. In 1229 Bishop Bingham built a bridge to the island in the middle of the river and erected a chapel dedicated to St John Baptist there. A chantry certificate of 1548 noted that Richard Eston of Winterbourne Dauntsey

had defaced the chapel and sold its tiles. The island is still known as St John's Isle, and the remains of the chapel are now incorporated into a private house. Bishop Bingham also enlarged and rearranged the hospital itself in 1244. It had two chapels at its east end, one dedicated to St Nicholas and the northern one to St Mary the Virgin. These were separated by an arcade of arches. It is thought that one of these was for men and the other for women. At the end of the 15th century much of the main building was pulled down, leaving only the chapels which still stand today. St Nicholas' Chapel, reconsecrated in 1501, is in daily use for services while St Mary's was adapted for other purposes in 1498. In 1675 the chapel was wainscoted and in 1695 the ancient colonnade of arches was walled in. The chapel was restored after a fire in 1855. In 1993 a new vestry was established and extra seating provided. The tiles in the sanctuary are 14th century and the chapel bell dates from 1623. This chapel underwent major structural restoration in 2007, the plaster being removed from the walls to reveal the original stonework. The decorated beams have also been cleaned.

Pelly. Hallett 7, 52. Howson 40, 41. Howson* 78–80, 144.

Trinity Hospital.

A small courtyard and chapel originally founded in 1390 were rebuilt *c.*1702 and restored to mark the 600th anniversary in 1990. The altar has its original 'mensa' stone, and the woodwork below displays intricate symbolic carvings. An inscription on the pews dates them to 1702 and is thought to refer to the Beckham family,

S

who were joiners in Salisbury. The original papal bull of Pope Boniface establishing Trinity Hospital can be seen in the board room.

Hallett 29, 59. Howson 112, 120. Howson* 145.

SALTAIRE, West Yorkshire

Model Village Almshouses.

Of the 850 dwellings built in 1853 by Sir Titus Salt, 45 were almshouses. A chapel was provided, but this has since been converted into a dwelling.

Howson 145–6. Corry.

SANDWICH, Kent

St Bartholomew's Hospital.

The hospital was probably founded in 1217 to commemorate the defeat of the French in that year. The foundation provided that three priests should officiate constantly in the chapel. The hospital survived the Dissolution.

Howson* 126. Website.

SHEFFIELD, West Yorkshire

The Earl of Shrewsbury Hospital.

The hospital with its chapel was built in Sheffield town centre in 1673 in accordance with the will of Gilbert Talbot, 7th Earl of Shrewsbury. In 1823 the hospital was rebuilt in Norfolk Road, in the fashionable Gothic style of the time. The arms of the Earl of Shrewsbury are to be seen in the windows. Portraits of the earl, together with his original letter of bequest, are in the large ante-chapel which is separated from the nave by a magnificently carved wooden screen. The bell once hung at Derwent Hall, and was presented to the chapel in 1956.

Website.

SHERBORNE, Dorset

The Almshouses of St John the Baptist and St John the Evangelist.

These almshouses were originally founded in 1406. The present foundation dates from 1437, and the chapel was consecrated in 1442. The original building is in the form of a monastic infirmary with a high eastern chapel. The residents of the almshouses were expected to attend Mass and Evensong daily in the chapel. The house escaped dissolution at the time of the Reformation because it was a charitable institution governed by a lay corporation. The chapel is entered through a high Perpendicular arch, and is separated from the ante-chapel by an open oak screen. The chapel is open to the men's dormitory above, so that the sick might hear Mass from their beds. The triptych behind the altar dates from *c*.1480. It is painted in oils on wooden panels, and depicts five of the miracles of Christ. It is thought to be northern French, possibly a copy of a lost picture by Van der Weyden. The large south window contains fine medieval glass. Copies of an illuminated

Above: The Almshouses of St John the Baptist and St John the Evangelist, Sherborne, Dorset.

Below: Triptych behind the chapel altar, Almshouses of St John the Baptist and St John the Evangelist.

S

royal licence and of the foundation deed are displayed in the ante-chapel. A service is held in the chapel each week.

Gibb. Howson* 82, 83, 119. Pl.7.

SHERBURN, Durham

Christ's Hospital in Sherburn.

The charity with its chapel was founded by Bishop Hugh Pudsey in 1181. Its foundation charter mentions that the hospital has a church and an inner chapel dedicated to St Nicholas. There was also an altar of St Mary Magdalene to which two priests were assigned. The chapel was destroyed by the Scots in 1300. In 1316 Bishop Kellan appointed another priest to serve 'in the new chapel which has been constructed in honour of the Blessed Virgin on the north side of the greater chapel.' The chapel is used as a district church for the area of Whitwell House as well as by the occupants of the hospital. The south wall of the nave and the lower part of the tower are original. The

Right and below:
Exterior and interior, Christ's Hospital in Sherburn, Durham.

windows, sedilia, and double piscina have been partially restored. The chancel only was originally stalled. Nave seating was introduced in the 19th century. The chapel was damaged by fire in 1866 and rebuilt in 1868. The arcading is from the 13th century. A brass plate in the sanctuary floor commemorates Thomas Leaver, Master from 1562. A chalice is dated 1564–5, and the paten and flagon are from 1712. There is a 17th-century chair in the sanctuary. The chapel possesses an icon of St Nicholas. The organ is by Harrison & Harrison of Durham. There is one bell in the tower, cast in 1724. Services are regularly held in the chapel, as well as at Beddell House Residential Care Home.

Gibby 3, 8, 11, 12, 30. University of Durham. Ryder. Massey. Prospectus.

S

SHOREDITCH, London

The Geffrye Almshouses.

These former almshouses of 1710 are now the Geffrye Museum. The chapel was originally conceived as a Great Room for meetings of the Charity Committee, but it was converted into a chapel in 1716. The four-tiered pulpit was flanked by two box pews with free-standing pews (one of which survives) being used within the main body of the space. An apse which accommodated the altar was added at the end of the 18th century. Three wall panels were uncovered in the apse during restoration in 1971. Two of them, bearing the text of the Creed and the Commandments, are original. The central panel bearing the text of the Lord's Prayer is a replica. A statue of the founder, Sir Robert Geffrye, stands in the niche above the doorway to the chapel which with its pediment and bell tower occupies the centre of the main range. His monument is on the wall of the chapel and his tomb is in the graveyard.

Haslam 5, 10–11. Hallett 59. Howson 112. Howson* 52.

SHORNE, Kent

St Katherine's Hospital.

The hospital was founded in the 14th century. The chapel is of flint banded with stone and has a piscina.

Howson* 126. Website.

SLEAFORD, Lincolnshire

Carre's Hospital.

The Hospital was founded in 1636 by Robert Carre. When the building was re-fronted in 1823 in Tudor style by Charles Kirk a chapel was added, but this was taken down and replaced by the present chapel in 1844. The chapel, which is unconsecrated, is in the centre of the south range with a pointed bell gable bearing the Carre coat of arms. It has not been used as a chapel since the 1950s, at a time when the bedesmen still wore a uniform. There was a weekly service and the men took it in turns to ring the bell for worship. A curate from the parish church took the services. Although unused, the chapel still contains some pews.

Howson* 129. Website. Alcock.

SOUTHAMPTON, Hampshire

The Hospital of St Julien (God's House).

The hospital was founded *c.*1197 by Gervaise le Riche. The Provost and

Left: The Geffrye Almshouses, 19th-century illustration. In 1914, the almshouses were converted to become the Geffrye Museum of the Home.

Fellows of Queen's Hospital, Oxford were appointed as perpetual warden in 1344. In 1462 Edward IV granted to the Warden, chaplains and brothers of God's House the alien priory of Sherborne, with the object of securing the increase of divine worship within the Hospital of St Julien or God's House and perpetual masses for the souls of the King and his successors, and for the souls of Richard, late Duke of York and Richard, late Earl of Cambridge, 'our grandfather who lies buried within the hospital'. The church or chapel of the house was dedicated to St Julien, and hence the hospital itself occasionally went by that name. The *Valor* of 1535 recorded payment of £1.13.4 for wax, wine and bread for the chapel. The chapel was for some time used by the Huguenot community. The old buildings were swept away and the present buildings erected in 1861. The chapel of St Julien has been extensively restored and occupies one side of the quadrangle.

Howson* 121. Doubleday & Page 202–5.

SOUTHBROOM, Wiltshire

The Hospital of St James and St Denis.
The leper hospital is said to have been founded by a Bishop of Salisbury. In 1232 Henry III granted wood from Melksham Forest for the building of a chapel. No references found after the 14th century, but a house near St James's Church originally named Spitalcroft seems to preserve the memory of the hospital.

Pugh & Crittall 362. Website.

Right: Original glass from the chapel of the Hospital of William Browne, Stamford, Lincolnshire.

SOUTHWARK, London

Drapers' Almshouses Chapel.
The chapel was built in Blackman Street in 1651 by John Walter, Citizen and Draper of London. Morning Prayer was being said daily in 1722.

Website.

The Licensed Victuallers' Benevolent Institute.
This was founded in 1827 and the buildings, designed by Henry Rose, were completed in 1828. They include a monumental stucco chapel with a hexastyle Ionic portico, pediment and belfry. The pediment has 'Founded 1827' in the tympanum either side of the clock with a classical cupola above. The interior of the chapel was destroyed in World War II and is now derelict.

Howson* 131. Website.

STAMFORD, Lincolnshire

The Hospital of William Browne.
The hospital was founded in 1475 with its own chapel where the bedesmen were required to attend the services twice daily, although they went to the nearby church of All Sts on Sundays. At the west end are a 15th-century screen and a row of original

Above and left: The Hospital of William Browne.

stalls with carved misericords. The altar
slab is of Barnack ragstone and bears its
five consecration crosses. It was hidden for
protection and restored to its place in 1925.
There is a 15th-century cope chair with a
semi-circular back. The reredos was painted
in 1919. The altar ornaments of silver on
steel were provided in 1963 and are now laid
up in the museum upstairs. The windows
contain coloured and white glass dating
from the 15th century, believed to have been
made by Henry VII's own glass maker; they
were restored in 1869 and 1967. As well
as figures of the Virgin Mary, the Sts and
the Holy Trinity can be seen the arms of
Browne, Stokke and Elmes.

Hoskins/Newton/King 3, 8-15. Sharp. Crust 9, 10, 12,
20, 47, 68, 69. Hallett 6. Howson 62. Howson* 100–1,
128. Pl.14.

Above and right:
Convocation room and (right) chapel interiors at the Hospital of William Browne.

S

Lord Burghley's Hospital.
The hospital incorporates some of the buildings of the 12th-century Hospital of St Thomas and St John. It was endowed by Lord Burghley in 1597. The chapel, on the other level, is now used as office accommodation, but its small tower and bell are still visible.

STOKE POGES, Buckinghamshire
Stoke Poges Hospital.
Founded in 1557 by Lord Edward Hastings near St Giles' Church. In 1558 the Hastings Chapel was built in red brick with stone mullioned windows on the outside of the church in the angle of the chancel and the south side as the oratory where the inmates of the almshouse could say prayers for their founder, and eventually as his burial place. The original almshouse was demolished and rebuilt *c.*1765, but was sold in 1947. The sculptured arms of Lord Hastings can be seen over the entrance door to the Hastings Chapel.
Howson 113. Website.*

STONEY STRATFORD, Buckinghamshire
Mr Fegan's Homes.
Founded in 1863 with a chapel to the front. The chapel has a rose window.
Howson 113.*

STRATFORD-UPON-AVON, Warwickshire
Guild Chapel of the Holy Cross.
The Fraternity or Guild of the Holy Cross was already in existence in 1269 when Bishop Godfrey Giffard of Worcester granted a licence to the brethren of the

Left: Guild Chapel of the Holy Cross, Stratford-upon-Avon, Warwickshire.

Guild to build a chapel and to found a hospital for the poor priests of the diocese. The present fabric of the chancel of the chapel incorporates portions of the original building, but the nave and tower were added in the 15th century by Sir Hugh Clopton. Following the suppression of the Guild at the Reformation, the chapel was confiscated by the Crown until 1553 when it was granted to the newly chartered Corporation of Stratford-upon-Avon. In 1804 a series of 15th-century wall paintings was discovered during building work in the chancel. The paintings had been defaced, painted over and hidden from sight since 1563. They were subsequently destroyed during the building work. In 1955 fragmentary remains of wall paintings in the nave were discovered and recorded by Wilfred Puddephat including a depiction of 'The Dance of Death' and a large scene of 'Doom or Judgment Day' above the chancel arch.
Website.

S

SWINGFIELD, Kent

St John's Commandery.

The Commandery belonged to the Knights of St John Hospitaller. This medieval building is of flint and served as both a chapel and hall for a chapter of the order. The medieval chapel was converted into a farm building during the 15th century. It features a striking timber roof and an ornamental plaster ceiling.

Website.

TADDIPORT, Devon

The Leper Hospital.

The first definite reference to the leper hospital is in 1418, but its chantry chapel of St Mary Magdalen is known to have existed in 1311, when Sir Richard de Brent was instituted as its chaplain. It was repaired with the blessing of the Pope in 1400. The commissioners of Edward VI reported in 1554 that 'The free chapel there founded by the awncestors of John Seyntledger, to th'intent that a pryst should say masse one day in ye weke to ye poore folks of ye sayd hospital and vysyte them in sickness'. In 1645 the chapel was provided with a bell cast by John Pennington of Exeter. In 1665, Tristram Arscott, the sole and perpetual guardian of the hospital, conveyed it to the Mayor and Burgesses of Great Torrington and the Church Wardens and Overseers of Little Torrington on condition that the chapel should be kept in good repair and that services should be held there regularly. All the hospital buildings with the exception of the chapel had disappeared by 1900. The chapel has a small embattled tower at the west end and a transept to the north east which is thought to be the oldest part of the building. The east window is modern but entirely in keeping. The south doorway is of later date, the original one having been further west, and a mullioned domestic window has been inserted over it in the 17th century. There are two other square-headed windows, and on the south side an 18th-century circular-headed window. The whole chapel is tiny, the tower measuring only five feet square and the nave being only thirty feet long. Services are still held each Sunday.

Howson* 118. Cresswell. Website.

TAMWORTH, Staffordshire

The Hospital of St James.

The hospital was founded by Sir Philip Marmion of Middleton Hall between 1266 and 1275. It is built of the same stone as the hall, and may originally have been a chantry chapel. A chaplain was appointed in 1283. Sir Henry Willoughby visited the hospital chapel to make his confession in 1524. The hospital was suppressed in 1548 when the chapel and its lands were sold. By the end of the 18th century the chapel had been turned into a barn, and subsequently it became a dwelling house. In 1855 the Brethren of the Guild of St Alban attempted to establish a monastic community in the chapel, which was by now ruined, but this failed and the chapel became a house once more. It was restored from 1909 and rededicated by the Bishop of Lichfield in 1914 to serve as a mission church in the Parish of Wigginton. The roof and walls were extensively restored in 2000. Services according to the 1662 Book of Common Prayer are regularly held in the chapel.

Website.

T

TAUNTON, Devon

Gray's Almshouses.

The almshouses were founded by Robert Gray in 1635. The chapel contains Gray's portrait and coat of arms. It was used for prayers, meetings of the residents and for the payment of pensions from the large oak chest in the centre of the room. It now contains old bibles. The chapel has its original benches and painted ceiling. An inscription on the outside of the building records that 'dailie prayers' constitute part of the maintenance prescribed for the 'tenne poore' residents.

Website.

TEMPLE BALSALL, Warwickshire

The Foundation of Lady Katherine Leveson.

The church of St Mary was built before 1330 with a large nave, chancel and sanctuary. Originally it was the chapel of the Knights Hospitaller who had succeeded the Knights Templar at the adjacent Old Hall. When the Knights left in the 1470s the church fell into disuse. It was restored in the second half of the 17th century and more extensively in the mid-19th century when Sir George Gilbert Scott returned it to something like its original medieval appearance. At this time it was given the

Below: The chapel at the Foundation of Lady Katherine Leveson, Temple Balsall, restored by George Gilbert Scott in the mid-19th century.

T

status of a parish church. In the meantime Lady Katherine Leveson, who died in 1674, had endowed a hospital or almshouse and a free school at Temple Balsall. The minister of the church was to be Master of the hospital and teacher at the school. To the present day the church scrvcs as chapel of the almshouses and as parish church, the Master also being the incumbent. The stalls assigned to the Governors and Almspeople of the Foundation of Lady Katherine Leveson stand in the chancel. A 14th-century Easter sepulchre is to be seen in the sanctuary. The east window of 1907 depicts scenes from the life of Christ culminating in the Ascension, together with the coats of arms of those associated with the church and the Foundation. The west end of the church has a rose window. The font of 1663 was replaced by a new one in 1846, but the original font has been recovered and was restored to its place in 1985. The church possesses a substantial quantity of plate, some of it dating from the foundation of the hospital. There is a tankard, a silver gilt chalice, paten and flagon of 1678, and a chalice of 1727.

Fairbairn. Gooder. Houlden. Hallett 59. Roche.

THORNTON-LE-DALE, North Yorkshire

Lady Lumley's Almshouses.
These were founded in 1657 by deed of Viscountess Lumley. The chapel at the east end, detached from the almshouses, is now used as a school. This has three bays, a stone cornice and a small bell in the end gable. The east window is pointed and of three lights of Perpendicular character.

The windows in the east and north sides are of two lights (one in the west) and transomed. The door is in the east wall. The building has a flat plaster ceiling coved at the sides.

Howson* 147. Page 492, 497. Website.

TIVERTON, Devon

Greenway's Almshouses.
Founded by John Greenway in the 1520s. A single-cell, three-bay chapel is attached to the west end of the almshouse block, fronting the street. This chapel was once a richly decorated structure with similarities to the Greenway Chapel at the Church of St Peter. It has opposed north and south doors towards the west end. The roof is of the 19th century with moulded ribs and flat carved bosses at the intersections. The pews, reading desk and seat are of the 1860s. The chapel was ornamented in 1783 and 1784 after most of it had been destroyed by fire. In the chapel there is an inscription asking the almshouse inhabitants to 'Have grace ye men and ever pray For the sowle of John and Joane Greenway.'

Howson* 118. Website. Fathi.

Waldron Almshouses.
The almshouses, founded in 1579, have an attached chapel with a porch. The building of this chapel was begun by John Waldron and completed by his widow in 1580 'for God to Prayse'. The almshouses and chapel were restored in 1990. The chapel bell, older than the chapel, was cast in 1539 and it is believed that John Waldron purchased it while on business in Cleves in Germany.

Howson* 118. Website. Fathi.

T

WALTON-ON-THAMES, Surrey

Whiteley Village.

The Village was founded by William Whiteley, who left £1 million in his will of 1907 to build homes for the indigent elderly. The chairman of the Trustees, the Bishop of London, felt most strongly that it would be the wish of the founder that a church or chapel should be built within the confines of the village. The church was dedicated on 25 April 1918, St Mark's Day, and given St Mark as its Patron. The church is in an elevated position and large in dimension, with vestries in the crypt. It has a central square tower. There are stained glass windows, depicting St Mark and the Baptism of Jesus. In 1947 silver was collected and melted down to make a chalice for the church. Among the donated memorial gifts are a chaplain's desk, a lectern and a portable font. In the 1990s the crypt was flooded, causing damage to the cupboards and robes in the vestry. A new window was installed to mark the millennium in 2000. The organ is an outstanding instrument by Norman & Beard, and its casework is by Walter Tapper. The village has a full-time chaplain. Services are regularly held and well attended.

A chapel of ease in the grounds of St Mark's Church was used as a Roman Catholic Church until 1993, when the Roman Catholic community was granted the use of an aisle in St Mark's itself. The chapel of ease still bears the outward decoration of a Roman Catholic church although it has been unused for some time and it is hoped that it will shortly be re-opened as a museum.

The Sanctuary, a free-standing brick building situated in a pleasant wooded area,

Left: Whitely Village, Walton-on-Thames.

W

serves as the United Free Church. Its first service was held on 20 May 1926. There is an inscription in Greek on the reredos. The building is spacious and light, with clear windows.

Weavey 100–3. Howson 71. Kimmins.*

WARWICK, Warwickshire

Lord Leycester's Hospital.

Right: West front of St James the Great, Lord Leycester's Hospital, Warwick.

Below: View from the east, Lord Leycester's Hospital, built over Warwick's West Gate.

The chantry chapel of St James the Great over the arched vaulting of Warwick's West Gate was built by Roger de Newburgh, second Norman Earl of Warwick, in 1126. In the late 14th century Thomas Beauchamp, 12th Earl of Warwick, restored it. It was granted to the Guild of St George in 1383 and has been in continuous

W

use ever since. The Guild of St George subsequently joined with the Guild of the Blessed Virgin and the Guild of the Holy Trinity to form the United Guilds of Warwick. They built a Guildhall, a Great Hall and other buildings adjacent to the chapel. When Henry VIII disbanded the united guilds in 1546 their buildings might well have been lost to the crown. However, the Master of the United Guilds, Thomas Oken, transferred ownership of the property at Westgate to the Burgesses of Warwick. In 1571 Robert Dudley, Earl of Leicester, close friend of Queen Elizabeth I, took over the buildings and in them set up his 'Hospital', a retirement home for old soldiers disabled in the service of the Queen. The establishment was headed by a Master (a Clerk in Holy Orders) and comprised twelve 'Brothers' and their wives. Dudley drew up a list of statutes and Queen Elizabeth passed an Act of Parliament setting up the Hospital. The hospital buildings were modernised in 1966. On weekday mornings the Brethren still gather in the chapel for prayers in the words laid down by the Founder in 1571, surrounded by fine examples of Warwick's celebrated tradition of woodcarving.

*Corry. Hallett 60. Howson*35, Pl.11. Lesinski.*

WELL, North Yorkshire
Well United Charities.
The almshouses were founded in 1578. The chapel, no longer in use, was rebuilt from the stones of a medieval hospital. It has a round-arched doorway.

Corry. Howson 148. Pevsner 1966: 381.*

WELLS, Somerset
Bishop Bubwith's Hospital.
The hospital of St Saviour was founded in 1424 under the will of Bishop Nicholas Bubwith. Its indenture was drawn up in 1836. There is a chapel at its eastern end.

Howson 40, 42, 48. Howson 81, 139. Scrase 51–2, 56.*

WESTBURY-ON-TRYM, Bristol
The St Monica Trust.
The almshouses possess a magnificent chapel built in 1919. This contains a 3–manual Willis organ, and the building is often used for concerts, taking advantage of its excellent acoustic.

Website.

WESTMINSTER, London
St Margaret's Almshouses.
These almshouses with their school and chapel were founded in 1566 by the Reverend Edward Palmer.

Website.

WEST STOCKWITH, Nottinghamshire
William Huntington Almshouses.
In 1715 William Huntington bequested £740 for the erection of a chapel and 10 almshouses in his shipyard. The chapel was built in 1722 with a house and six acres of land. It is dedicated to St Mary and was restored and re-seated in 1887. It is in the Perpendicular style and consists of chancel, nave and bell turret.

Website.

W

WILTON, Wiltshire

The Hospital of St Giles & St Anthony.
This hospital was founded for lepers by Adele of Louvain, second wife of Henry I, *c*.1135. The tradition that she herself was a leper and was buried in the chapel appears to be without foundation. In 1301 the chapel was receiving £4 per annum of the King's gift, to provide a chaplain who celebrated Mass daily in the chapel for the souls of the Kings of England. In 1385 Richard II sent an aged servant to be one of the King's 13 poor bedesmen (oratorum) of St Giles' hospital. In 1403 William Chitterne of Wilton had licence to grant 12.5 acres in Fugglestone, Chilhampton and South Newton, to find a lamp to burn daily at High Mass in the hospital chapel. The commissioners of 1548 found a chapel with a lead-covered roof and four poor persons relieved. After 1830 the site was demolished and new almshouses built in the Warminster Road.

Pugh/Crittall 362–4. Website.

Below: The Hospital of St John the Baptist, Wilton.

The Hospital of St John the Baptist.
The hospital is first mentioned in 1195, and its chapel was dedicated in 1217. In 1318 and 1335 Richard of Chisledon granted lands to the hospital to find a chaplain to celebrate Mass daily in the hospital church for the souls of his family.

The prior and convent engaged a priest in 1395 and provided for his maintenance. A chaplain was still found in office by the commissioners in 1546, and the hospital survived the Dissolution. It was described as decaying in 1825. The buildings were rebuilt in 1851. The chapel was restored

Above: Interior of the 15th-century chapel at St John's Winchester Charity. The armorial glass was donated by the Devenish family.

W

in 1868 and enlarged *c.*1902. The present buildings are of flint and stone with some red brick patching. The chapel was extensively refurbished and restored in the 1980s and again in 2012. It still serves as the focal point for the Almshouse community of St John's Hospital, comprising some twenty residents, together with a further twelve residents from the College of Matrons, whose main base is in Salisbury Cathedral Close. A Eucharist service is conducted weekly by the Chaplain, a post customarily held ex-officio by the Rector of Wilton.

Pugh/Crittall 364-7. Website. O'Connor.

WIMBORNE, Dorset

St Margaret' & Stone's Almshouses.

The chapel, together with at least three of the almshouses, one of which was the priest's house, dates from the 12th century when it was a leper hospital. It was re-founded by John of Gaunt in 1241. In the mid-17th century the management was assumed by the Bankes family, which owned the adjoining Kingston Lacy estate. The chapel, dedicated to God, St Margaret and St Anthony, has a waggon roof. It has survived a series of times of neglect and rebirth, and was re-opened in 1885 by the efforts of the Revd F.W. Fairbank, Curate of Wymbourneminster. It was renovated in 1900, when the murals on the south wall were painted out, and severely restored in the 1970s. There are a number of documents extant relating to its use. The chapel contains a harmonium originating from Ann Arbor, Michigan.

Booklet. Lock. Howson 119.*

WIMBORNE St GILES, Dorset

Sir Anthony Ashley's Almshouses.

Founded in 1627 with a central chapel.

Howson 119.*

WINCHESTER, Hampshire

St John's Winchester Charity.

The first chapel on the site was built to serve the Hospital of St John, founded by St Brinstan in 931–34. A further chapel may have been added in 1332. The present chapel dates from 1428. It was converted into a school in 1710 but restored by G.E. Street in 1838 and reordered in 1909. On the south wall are pictures of St Jerome, St Giles, St John the Baptist and St Blaise. Several coats of arms are to be seen in the windows. The 16th-century armorial glass was originally in the Devenishs' house in Sussex. The Devenish family also donated the east window, which depicts the Good Shepherd, John the Baptist, Isaiah and St John the Evangelist. The lambs in the window are thought to refer to Ralph Lamb, who restored the foundation by building six almshouses in 1554. On the north wall hangs a copy by Dura of *The Holy Family* by Raphael. The charity employs a chaplain, and services take place in the chapel on Sundays and Wednesdays.

Carpenter-Turner. Leaflets. Howson 78, 81, 121.*

The Hospital of St Cross.

The hospital was founded by Henry de Blois between 1133 and 1136. The fine Transitional Norman church, begun *c.*1135 and completed in 1295, is the only major survival from the hospital's earliest days. It was originally thatched, until a lead roof was supplied between 1335 and

1345. The west window and the clerestory windows date from the same period, and later in the 14th century the tower was raised and the choir was re-roofed. The medieval encaustic tiles date from *c*.1390. Traces of wall paintings in the south transept are the last remains of what was once an altar to St Thomas of Canterbury. The Norman font and stone screens were brought from the neighbouring church of St Faith, demolished in 1507. The ornate woodcarving in the choir is thought to have come from Wolvesey Palace. The Lady Chapel has a Flemish triptych from *c*.1520, and contains the Beaufort Chair used at the Gowning Ceremony of the Brothers. The lectern, carved between 1400 and 1500, has the head of a parrot (a warning against repeating the scriptures in parrot fashion) and on its head a heart (signifying the love of Christ). During the Commonwealth this was buried in St Faith's churchyard and replaced in the church at the Restoration.

The 14th-century altar stone was also buried beneath the altar, and was restored to its former position only in 1928. The stone carving around the windows varies in character from one window to another. Particularly striking is the 'bird's beak' pattern in the north transept. The brothers of the original foundation (black gown) and the Brothers of the Order of Noble Poverty (red gown) attend morning service daily. The church also serves as the parish church of the Parish of St Cross and St Faith.

Hopewell. Mcilwain. Hallett 28, 61. Howson 57–60. Howson* 95, 96, 121.

WOKINGHAM, Buckinghamshire
The Henry Lucas Hospital.

This was founded by the will of Henry Lucas in 1663 with a chaplain as its Master. The buildings, possibly designed by Sir Christopher Wren, were completed and the chapel was consecrated in 1666. The chapel contains two stained glass windows. In 2001

W

the charity merged with Whiteley Village
and the buildings were sold into private
hands.

Website.

WOODBRIDGE, Suffolk

The Seckford Foundation.

Thomas Seckford (1515–87) was a
Member of Parliament, a wealthy lawyer
and successful merchant. When Queen
Elizabeth I transferred responsibility
for the poor onto wealthy landowners,
businessmen and lawyers, Thomas Seckford
accepted this responsibility. In 1587 he was
granted a royal licence to build and endow
almshouses in Woodbridge. The present
Seckford Hospital was erected in 1834
and designed by C.R. Cockerel. The small
chapel is at the heart of this 19th-century
foundation and is regularly used for worship
led by the clergy of St Mary's parish in
Woodbridge. The internal corridor of the
almshouses is now formed around the nave,

so that the stained glass windows can be seen from inside the building on the first floor. An internal ramp has been created to facilitate access to the chapel from inside the building; previously, access was via the external cloisters only. There is evidence that services have been held in this chapel since the 1900s. The organ dates from 1906, and there are historical registers in the Seckford archives recording the tenants' attendance.

Kopferschmitt.

WOOTTON-UNDER-EDGE, Gloucestershire

Perry's Almshouses.

These almshouses, founded under the Will of Hugh Perry, who died in 1634, were built in 1638. An Usher was appointed to read Divine Service daily in the chapel. When the Thomas Dawes Hospital was founded in 1723, an arrangement was made by which the new hospital might share the chapel and other facilities with Perry's Almshouses. Subsequently this arrangement was extended to the General Hospital Foundation. Weekly services are now held at the chapel.

Hallett 27, 61. Website. Leaflet.

WORCESTER, Worcestershire

The Hospital of St Wulstan.

The original foundation dates from before Bishop Wulstan's death in 1095. A Master, two chaplains and several lay brothers and sisters offered aid to pilgrims, the poor and the sick. In 1294 William de Molendis made a donation to the hospital in return for masses and prayers in the chapel. The present buildings of the hospital date from the 15th century. In 1441 Bishop Bouchier laid down that the brethren

and sisters should join daily in prayers for the souls of their predecessors. The hospital was suppressed in 1540 and given over to residential use and, latterly, as a Commandery. The base of a pillar from an original chapel of St Godwald is visible and has recently been excavated. The main building is now a museum, and the site of the chapel is occupied by kitchens and by a separate house.

Howson* 24, 26. Leaflet.

The Hospital of St Oswald.

According to Leland, the house was 'first erected for monks then infected with leprosy', then later turned into a hospital. Its foundation is traditionally attributed to St Oswald of York (Bishop of Worcester 961–72). In 1334 a grant of 100 acres was made on condition that two chaplains were provided to celebrate divine service for the soul of the King and Queen Philippa. In 1539 the hospital, with its chapel and churchyard, was leased to John Hereford, so escaping complete dissolution. The advowson of the chapel was granted in 1542 to the Dean and Chapter of Worcester. The hospital was re-founded and extended in the 17th century. In 1873 the buildings were destroyed, and entirely new ones erected in the Gothic style.

Willis-Bund/Page 175–9. Website.

Berkeley's Hospital.

This was endowed in 1692 by Robert Berkeley. It is built in brick with stone dressings. At the top of the court is the chapel, entered by a doorway over which are the Berkeley arms and in a niche the figure of the founder dated 1703. The chapel

W

Above: The 17th-century façade of the chapel, Berkeley's Hospital, Worcester.

has five bays with arched windows, a large doorway, a hipped roof and lantern. The fittings were removed in 1867.

Howson 121. Pevsner 1968: 332.*

Laslett's Almshouses.

These almshouses were founded by William Laslett in 1868. A chapel was also built for the use of the public as well as of the inmates, the chaplain receiving £60 a year. The almshouses were rebuilt in 1911–12. Their main range contains the central free Perpendicular-style chapel flanked by the boardroom and chaplain's house.

Website.

The Trinity Chapel.

This stood at the rear of St Nicholas' Church. It was suppressed by Edward VI, and an almshouse, endowed by Queen Elizabeth I, was founded on the site. The present buildings are modern.

Website.

YORK, North Yorkshire

Lady Hewley's Almshouses.

A group of almshouses originally founded in 1700 by Dame Sarah Hewley with a chapel at the rear. When the site was required for railway construction the almshouses were removed to their present position in St Saviourgate in 1840, with a tiny chapel built into a corner of the cottages. This was converted into a dwelling in 1975.

Howson 143. Corry. Howson 65, 148. Nuttgens 236. Smith 99–101.*

Y

The Merchant Adventurers' Hall.

The Undercroft of the Hall (1357) was used as a hospital for the poor and infirm citizens of York. A simple chapel was provided, and two chaplains are known to have been serving there in 1396. A new chapel was built in 1411, so arranged that the sick in the undercroft could see the chapel altar. It once had three altars, statues of Sts and other costly furnishings. The windows were repaired by William Cleveland in 1490. The furnishings were removed at the Reformation in 1549, but worship in the chapel continued. In 1644 Thomas Herbert endowed an annual sermon, which is still preached in the chapel at Michaelmas. The chapel was refurbished in 1677, refurnished in 1669, and refurbished again in 1797. There are painted boards on the walls, one of which displays the Merchant Adventurers' Prayer whilst others give details of repairs to the chapel. The remains of the ancient chapel were excavated in 1949. The present cross and candlesticks date from the 1970s. The altar, dating from the 17th century, was brought to the chapel from the church of St Mary Walmgate in the 1980s. The original chapel silver has been dispersed, but the chapel possesses an Elizabethan Communion cup dating from 1568, which has been donated in modern times. There is also a modern silver alms dish. The glass and stained glass roundels and panels, one with a sundial, were set into the east window of the chapel in 1999 in memory of John Saville, a former Governor. There are Edwardian depictions of the

Right: Chapel interior, the Merchant Adventurers' Hall, York.

Left: Chapel interior from the east, the Merchant Adventurers' Hall, York.

company's seals in the south window. The chapel was dedicated to the Holy Trinity, which is depicted on the seal and in a statue on loan from the Priory Church of Holy Trinity, Micklegate. The medieval wooden screen remains.

Howson 31, 36. Corry. Howson* 33, Pl.3. Booklet 10, 11. Smith 80, 81. Hartshorne 18, 19, 112, 113, 123-7, 160-5. Marshall.

St Anthony's Hall.

The chapel of this foundation was originally dedicated to the Blessed Mary and St Martin when it was consecrated in 1453. It was accessed from the Aldwark side of the building. Stone niches remaining in the wall probably held statues of the Virgin Mary and St Martin. During the building's use as a hospital and a house of correction in the 17th century the chapel was divided into three rooms. The buildings later became a Bluecoat School, then a Diocesan Archive, and now a Quilt Museum and Gallery.

Howson 31. Corry. Rae 3, 4. Smith 86.

The Hospital of St Leonard.

Originally dedicated to St Peter when it was founded by King Athelstan in 986, the hospital was moved to its present site by William II, re-founded by Stephen in 1145 and dedicated to St Leonard. The ruins of the infirmary chapel still remain. Its bell tower was destroyed by fire in the 14th century, and the vestments had been sold by then. The hospital was finally suppressed at the Dissolution.

Howson 28, 35. Corry. Howson* 20. Nuttgens 152.

Ingram's Hospital.

This hospital was established by Sir Arthur Ingram in Bootham in 1630–32, utilising an old Norman archway dated *c.*1190 and purchased from Holy Trinity Priory. This stands below a square battlemented tower and serves as the entrance porch to the chapel. This small chapel was provided with an 'honest and able man' to read prayers there. The buildings were damaged in the siege of 1644 and rebuilt in 1649. Now in private hands, they still stand in Bootham, and the chapel, which was converted into a dwelling before 1900, is visible from the rear.

Nuttgens 189. Smith 29, 92.

The Hospital of St Mary Magdalene.

Burton's Cross, which also stands in Bootham, is thought to be a pillar, furnished with holy water stoups, from the medieval hospital of St Mary Magdalene which was dissolved and destroyed at the reformation.

The Common Hall.

This was the home of the Guild of St Christopher from 1456, and its 'maison dieu' was possibly housed in or under the chapel. The chapel by the 1720s had become a public house known as the Cross Keys. This site is now occupied by the Mansion House, and the Common Hall, restored after war damage in 1942, is now known as the Guildhall.

Smith 20, 66, 87.

Hestergate/Hertergate.

This hospital for the poor was founded by Thomas Howm in 1390 with an associated chantry chapel.

Smith 25.

Horsefair.

A hospital or chantry chapel dedicated to St Anne is thought to have been situated here.

Smith 25.

St Nicholas' Hospital.

The church of St Nicholas was founded between 1088 and 1112. The hospital was founded a little later following grants of land in 1132 and 1161. By the 14th century the hospital had declined, and was annexed to Holy Trinity Priory. The church continued in use as a parish church until 1644 when it was destroyed during the Civil War. Its doorways and bells were dispersed among other churches in York.

Smith 76, 77.

St Giles' Hospital.

This was probably founded around 1274 as a chapel of St Leonard's Hospital.

Smith 77.

St Helen's Hospital.

This was a leper hospital attached to a church dedicated to St Helen. It was demolished in 1622.

Smith 83.

Sir Thomas Hesketh's Hospital.

The hospital was originally established by Sir Thomas Hesketh and, after his death, by his wife Dame Julia, in 1608. After falling into penury and disrepair during the Civil War it was rebuilt on its present site on the Fulford Road by the squire, Henry Yarburgh, in 1795. This building originally had a chapel at its centre. The central pediment still bears an inscription which quotes Psalm 68.10.

Smith 89.

Wandesford's Hospital.

This was built in 1839 in accordance with the will of Mary Wandesford which provided for a Religious House to accommodate ten poor gentlewomen who were unmarried and practised the established religion. As such, it was provided with a chapel on the first floor, which is still used for monthly worship.

Smith 107–08.

Ann Harrison's Almshouses.

The original hospital was built in 1845. It had a central chapel, which was not used for worship after 1900. In 1964 new almshouses were built nearby to replace the original hospital which, being by now in bad repair and unsafe, was demolished.

Smith 112.

Y

Bibliography

Abbot's Hospital, *The Chapel Windows in the Hospital of the Blessed Trinity, Guildford.*

Alexander, M., *Abbot's Hospital: a Guide to the Hospital of the Blessed Trinity, Guildford,* Guildford 1999.

Ancient Guild Hall of the Company of Merchant Adventurers of the City of York, leaflet.

Ashbee, C.R., *The Trinity Hospital in Mile End: An Object Lesson in Ancient History,* 1896.

Askew, C., Information on Bradford Tradesmen's Homes supplied privately.

Barber, W.E., *Praise be to Marmaduke,* Ripon 2006.

Beese, A.K., *Coningsby Hospital,* Hereford 1971.

Benyon, C., Benyon, T., *Report on the Stained Glass Windows of Baptiste Sutton in Abbot's Hospital,* Hampton.

Binney, M., The Times, 2007.

Bold, J.,Bradbeer, C., van der Merwe, P., *Maritime Greenwich, a World Heritage Site,* rev.ed. 2002.

Bradford Tradesmen's Homes, *Annual Report 2006.*

Brooker, A. & Whiteman, M., *Saffron Walden, Portrait of a Market Town,* 1995.

Brown, J., *The French Hospital,* 2001.

Brownlee, C.R., Information on Beauchamp Almshouses supplied privately.

Carey, J., Information on Greyfriars Chapel supplied privately.

Carpenter-Turner, B., *St John's Winchester Charity,* Chichester 1992.

Chapel of St John the Baptist, Winchester, leaflet.

Chislett, D.V., *Sackville College, a Short History and Guide*, rev. ed. 2007.

Christ's Hospital in Sherburn, *Prospectus.*

Clayton, H., *St John's Hospital, Lichfield, A Short History.*

Colbourne, A., Information on the Crispe Almshouses supplied privately.

Collingwood, J., *Mr Saffron Walden - George Stacey Gibson 1818–1883*, 2008.

Collins, R., Information on Colston's Almshouses supplied privately.

Conwy County Council, leaflet on the Gwydir Almshouses.

Cooper, J., *The Well-Ordered Town 1792–1862*, 2000.

Corry, P.C., Research notes supplied privately.

Craig, J., Information on St Edmund's Hospital supplied privately.

Cresswell, B., *Little Torrington: The Church and Manor Lands and the Magdalen Hospital of Taddiport,* 1937.

Crust, L., *Lincolnshire Almshouses: Nine Centuries of Charitable Housing,* Sleaford 2002.

Dale, S., Information on Winsley's Charity supplied privately.

Deas, L.S., Information on the Charterhouse, Hull, supplied privately.

Doubleday, A.H. & Page, W., (ed.) *A History of the County of Hampshire, Vol.2,* 1973.

Doyle, C., Information on Kilmainham Hospital supplied privately.

Durham University, *The Chapel at Sherburn Hospital,* Archaeological Monitoring 1999.

Everett, M. & Stewart, D., *The Buildings of Saffron Walden,* 2003.

Fairbairn, F.R., *The Knights of the Temple & of St John of Jerusalem & their Connection with Temple Balsall,* repr. Temple Balsall 2002.

Farrell, J., Information on The Leathersellers' Almshouses supplied privately.

Fathi, L., Information on Greenway's Almshouses and Waldron's Almshouses supplied privately.

Fussell, P., Information on Drapers' Almshouses, Newington Butts, supplied privately.

Gaydon, A.T. & Pugh, A., *History of the County of Shropshire, Vol.2,* 1973.

Gibb, J.H.P., *The Almshouse of St John Baptist and St John Evangelist, Sherborne.*

Gibby, C.W., *Sherburn Hospital,* repr. 1998.

Gloucester Charities' Trust, *St Margaret's Chapel.*

Gooder, E., *Temple Balsall 1150–1870,* Temple Balsall, repr. 2002.

Goodman, N., *Eton College,* London 1976.

Goring Heath Charities, *History,* 1928.

Goring Heath Almshouses, leaflet and Chapel card.

Gough, Y.A., *A Short Guide to Bromley & Sheppard's Colleges,* 2004.

Grain, A.E., *The College of St Barnabas: A Guide to the Chapel,* 2007.

Granath, D., Information on The Hospital of God supplied privately.

Hallett, A., *Almshouses,* Princes Risborough 2004.

Hart, K.M., *The Conwy Valley and the Lands of History,* Ashbourne 2004.

Hartshorne, P., *The York Merchant Adventurers and their Hall,* London 2011.

Haslam, K., *A History of the Geffrye Almshouses,* London 2004.

Hayes, R., Pinnock, K., White, A. *Eastbridge Hospital.*

Hird, E., *The Lady Margaret Hungerford Almshouse and Free School, Corsham, Wiltshire, 1668–1968,* 2nd impression Corsham 2007.

Hobhouse, H. (ed.), *Survey of London, Vols 43 & 44: Poplar, Blackwall and Isle of Dogs,* 1994.

Hopewell, P., *Saint Cross - England's Oldest Almshouse,* Chichester 1995.

Hopkins, P., *The History of Beverley, East Yorkshire,* Pickering 2003.

Hoskins, J.P., Newton, P.A., & King, D. *The Hospital of William Browne, Merchant, Stamford, Lincolnshire,* Stamford.

Houlden, J.L., *The Church of St Mary the Virgin, Temple Balsall,* Temple Balsall 2004.

Howson, B., *Houses of Noble Poverty,* Sunbury-on-Thames 1993.

Howson*, B., *Almshouses: A Social & Architectural History,* Stroud 2008.

Hunnisett, J., Information on Huggens College supplied privately.

Ingram Hill, D., *The Ancient Hospitals and Almshouses of Canterbury,* rev. M. Lyle. Canterbury 2004.
— *St John Baptist, Northgate,* Ashford.
— *St Nicholas, Harbledown,* Ashford.

Irish Museum of Modern Art, *Guide.*

Jones, D., *John Foster's Almshouse and the Chapel of the Three Kings of Cologne,* 2004.

Jones, G.T., *The Chapel and Hospital of St Mary Magdalen, Ripon.*

Jones, N., Information on Trinity Almshouses, Mile End, supplied privately.

Joyce, J.B.A., Information on the Almshouses of the Holy Name, Hurstpierpoint, supplied privately.

Kimmins, B., *A Short History of St Mark's Church, Whiteley Village,* rev. 2010.

Kopferschmitt, S., Information on the Seckford Foundation supplied privately.

Lady Margaret Hungerford Charity, *Corsham Almshouses & 17th-century Schoolhouse.*

Lancaster Charity, *Almshouses.*

Leicester Archaeological Society, *Frolesworth.*

Lesinski, G., Information on Lord Leycester's Hospital supplied privately.

Linton-in-Craven in the Yorkshire Dales, *Fountaine's Hospital,* (leaflet).

Lock, N.M., Information on St Margaret's & Stones Almshouses supplied privately.

Macdougall, P., *The Story of Chichester,* 2004.

Manco, J., *The Spirit of Care: The Eight-Hundred-Year Story of St John's Hospital, Bath,* Bath 1998.

Marshall, L., Information on The Merchant Adventurers' Hall supplied privately.

Martin, M., *St Edmund's Chapel,* Gateshead.

Massey, H., *Sherburn Hospital, Sherburn, County Durham,* Archaeological Monitoring. Durham 2008.

Matthew, G.M., Information on the Hospital of St John & St Anne, Oakham, supplied privately.

Mcilwain, J., *The Hospital of St Cross and St Cross Church,* repr. Andover 1999.

Michael Yoakley's Charity, *Leaflet.*

Morden College Trustees, *Morden College: A Brief Guide,* rev. ed. 2006.

Munby, J., *St Mary's Hospital, Chichester, A Short History and Guide,* 1987.

National Trust, *The Holy Jesus Hospital.*

Nuttgens, P., *The History of York, Yorkshire,* Pickering 2007.

O'Connor, N., Information on the Hospital of St John Baptist, Wilton, supplied privately.

Page, W., *A History of the County of Kent, Vol. 2,* 1926.
— (ed.) *A History of the County of York, North Riding, Vol. 2,* 1923.
— (ed.) *A History of the County of York, Vol. 3,* 1974.

Parfitt, J.H., *Hugh Sexey's Hospital, Bruton.*

Partis College, *Brochure*

Paton, A., Information on the Sandham Memorial Chapel supplied privately.

Peel, M.J., *College of St Barnabas - Notes on the Verses and Texts in the Chapel Windows,* 1997.

Pelly, R., *The First Seven Centuries,* repr. as *The Story of St Nicholas' Hospital, Salisbury,* 1997.

Pevsner, N., *The Buildings of England – Yorkshire, North Riding,* Harmondsworth 1966.
— *The Buildings of England – Warwickshire,* rev. A. Wedgwood. Harmondsworth 1966.
— *The Buildings of England – Yorkshire, West Riding,* rev. E. Radcliffe. Harmondsworth 1967.
— *The Buildings of England – Cumberland & Westmoreland,* Harmondsworth 1967.
— *The Buildings of England – Worcestershire,* Harmondsworth 1968.
— *The Buildings of England – Hertfordshire,* rev. B. Cherry, Harmondsworth 1977.
— *The Buildings of England – Shropshire,* repr. New Haven & London 2002.
— *The Buildings of England – Derbyshire,* 2nd ed. rev. E.Williamson, repr. New Haven & London 2002.
— *The Buildings of England – Cheshire,* with E.Hubbard repr. New Haven & London 2003.
— *The Buildings of England – Lancashire: North,* rev. C. Hartwell, New Haven & London 2009.

Phillips, E., *A Short History of the Great Hospital, Norwich,* 1999.

Porter, S. & Richardson, H., *The Charterhouse: A Guide,* 2000.

— *The Savoy Manor: Hospital: Chapel.*

Prior, T., Information on Harvey's and Jubilee Homes supplied privately.

Pugh, R.B. & Crittall, E. *A History of the County of Wiltshire, Vol. 3,* 1956.

Rae, J., *A Brief History of St Anthony's Hall, Peasholme,* York.

Redhead, L., Information on Holy Jesus Hospital supplied privately.

Richards, I., Information on the Hospital of St John, Heytesbury, supplied privately.

Richmond, A., Information on Abbot's Hospital supplied privately.

Roche, S., Information on the Foundation of Lady Katherine Leveson supplied privately.

Roderick, T., Information on St Giles' Hospital and William Price's Almshouses supplied privately.

Ryder, P.F., *The Chapel, Sherburn Hospital, Durham. An Archaeological Assessment,* Durham 2001.

St Anne's Bedehouses, Sewell Road, Lincoln. Brochure.

St John's Winchester Charity, *Leaflet.*

St Margaret's Chapel, London Road, Gloucester, *Leaflet.*

St Margaret's & Stones Almshouses, 125th Anniversary booklet, 2010.

St Mary's Church, Ewelme, the Almshouse and the School. Guide.

St Mary's Homes, Godstone, *Leaflet.*

Salisbury Local History Group, *Caring: A History of Salisbury City Charities,* Salisbury 2000.

Scrase, T., *Wells, a Small City,* Stroud 2006.

Serjeantson, R.M. & Adkins, W.R.D., *A History of the County of Northampton Vol 2,* 1906.

Sharp, P., *The Hospital of William Browne, Stamford.*

Shepherd, V., Information on Faversham United Municipal Charities supplied privately.

Sir William Turner's Almshouses, *Leaflet.*

Smith, C., *The Almshouses of York,* York 2010.

Sotheran, P., *Sir William Turner and his Hospital at Kirkleatham,* 2001.

— *Sir William Turner's Almshouses, Kirkleatham,* Kirkleatham 2008.

Stewart, M., Information on the Frances Darlington Almshouses supplied privately.

Such, H., Information on the College of St Barnabas supplied privately.

Tancell, J., Information on Wyatt Almshouses supplied privately.

Taylor, B., *Abbot's Hospital, Guildford,* Guildford 1999.

Taylor, M., *The Greyfriars, Canterbury: the First Franciscan House in England,* Canterbury 2003.

Thawley, J., *A Certain Hospital Forever: A Recent History of Wyggeston's Hospital,* Leicester 1997.

Trinity House, *Guide.*

Vick, S.K.Ll., *The History of the Archbishop Holgate Hospital in Hemsworth 1555–2005 and the Life of its Founder Robert Holgate,* 2005.
— The Archbishop Holgate Hospital in Hemsworth in *Good News,* ACS 2005.

Vinnicombe, R., Information on Dr Milley's Hospital supplied privately.

Waite, R.C.F., Information on Trinity Hospital, Castle Rising, supplied privately.

Watts, S., *Shropshire Almshouses,* Woonton Almeley 2010.

Weavey, M., *Saga* Magazine, November 2008.

Willis-Bund, J.W. & Page, W., (ed.) *A History of the County of Worcester, Vol.2,* 1971.

Worcester City Council, *A Short Guide to the Commandery and its History.*

Worshipful Company of Drapers, *Queen Elizabeth's College, Greenwich.*

Youngs, M., *Notes on the Church of St Helen,* 1995.

ACKNOWLEDGEMENTS

Anthony De Ritter would like to thank Jacqueline Edmunds for her invaluable assistance in compiling this book.